KNIT SOXX

FOR EVERYONE

Published by Stackpole Books
An imprint of The Rowman & Littlefield Publishing Group, Inc.
4501 Forbes Blvd., Ste. 200
Lanham, MD 20706
www.stackpolebooks.com

Distributed by NATIONAL BOOK NETWORK
800-462-6420

The original German edition was published as *SoxxBook family + friends by Stine & Stitch*.
Copyright © 2018 frechverlag GmbH, Stuttgart, Germany (www.topp-kreativ.de)
This edition is published by arrangement with Claudia Böhme Rights & Literary Agency, Hannover, Germany
(www.agency-boehme.com)

PHOTOGRAPHS: frechverlag GmbH, 70499 Stuttgart, Germany; lichtpunkt, Michael Ruder, Stuttgart, Germany
PRODUCT MANAGEMENT: Mareike Upheber
EDITING: Regina Sidabras, Berlin, Germany
ILLUSTRATIONS: Josy Jones Graphic Design & Illustrations
LAYOUT: Petra Theilfarth
TRANSLATION: Katharina Sokiran

We have made every effort to ensure the accuracy and completeness of these instructions. We cannot, however,
be responsible for human error, typographical mistakes, or variations in individual work.

British Library Cataloguing in Publication Information available

Library of Congress Cataloging-in-Publication Data available
Names: Balke, Kerstin, author.
Title: Knit soxx for everyone : 25 colorful sock patterns for the whole
    family / Kerstin Balke.
Other titles: SoxxBook family + friends by Stine & Stitch
Description: Guilford, Connecticut : Stackpole Books, [2021], 2021. |
    Previously published: SoxxBook family + friends by Stine & Stitch.
    Stuttgart : frechverlag GmbH, 2018. | Summary: "In this new book,
    Kerstin Balke brings her signature colorful style to knit socks for men,
    women, and children. The 25 patterns feature eye-catching Fair Isle in
    color schemes ranging from brights that children will love to more muted
    and sophisticated styles for men and women"— Provided by publisher.
Identifiers: LCCN 2020049674 (print) | LCCN 2020049675 (ebook) | ISBN
    9780811739573 (paperback) | ISBN 9780811769563 (epub)
Subjects: LCSH: Knitting—Patterns. | Socks.
Classification: LCC TT825 .B2954 2021 (print) | LCC TT825 (ebook) | DDC
    746.43/2041—dc23
LC record available at https://lccn.loc.gov/2020049674
LC ebook record available at https://lccn.loc.gov/2020049675

♾️™ The paper used in this publication meets the minimum requirements of American National Standard for
Information Sciences—Permanence of Paper for Printed Library Materials, ANSI/NISO Z39.48-1992.

First Edition

KNIT SOXX

FOR EVERYONE

25 Colorful
Sock Patterns
FOR THE
WHOLE FAMILY

KERSTIN BALKE,
OF STINE 3 STITCH

STACKPOLE
BOOKS

Guilford, Connecticut

Let's Have a Soxx Party

You're My Soxx, You're My Soul

I'm Sailing in My Soxx

Soxx by Nature

Be-My-Valentine Soxx

From Big to Small

Basic Instructions

Sock-Knitting Love

I just love knitting socks, whether in stranded colorwork patterns, solid colored, or striped! For several years now, I've been blogging about this passion and have shown my socks on Instagram. It always fascinates me how different the same pattern can look in a different color scheme. I'm mightily happy when I can inspire creativity in my readers, and some of them knit colorwork and/or socks for the first time because of me.

With this book, I hope to be able to persuade you, too, to knit with several strands of yarn and in color. From small, patterned bands to all-over colorwork, covering the sock from cuff to toe, there's something for everybody. If you don't feel ready to venture into stranded knitting with two colors right now, you can start with simple striped socks and later continue with small colorwork patterns.

Since all sock patterns in this book have a pattern repeat of four stitches in width, every pattern fits every size, lending free rein to your creativity.

I wish you much fun when knitting socks!

Kerstin Balke

Let's Have a

Soxx Party »»»»»»»»»

SOXX 1

DIFFICULTY LEVEL 3

SIZES

Child's 1–10

Pattern instructions as given are for Child's 4–5, foot length approximately 5.9 in./15 cm. Changes to stitch counts and variations needed for other child sizes are given on page 13.

MATERIALS

Lang Yarns Jawoll, super fine (75% wool, 25% nylon; 230 yd./210 m; 1.75 oz./50 g), 1 skein each in #01 White, #159 Tangerine, and #220 Pastel Blue

DPNs, sizes US 1.5–2.5/2.5–3.0 mm

GAUGE

In colorwork pattern on US 1.5–2.5/2.5–3.0 mm needles, 34 sts and 38 rnds = 4 x 4 in./10 x 10 cm

>Let's Have a Soxx Party<

INSTRUCTIONS

CO 52 sts in Tangerine, distribute evenly onto 4 DPNs (13 sts per needle), and join into the round.

For the cuff, work 8 rnds (0.8 in./2 cm) in Cuff Ribbing pattern.

Work the leg in stockinette stitch, beginning with 2 rnds in White, and then continue in stranded pattern in White, Pastel Blue, and Tangerine. Work Rnds 1–6 of the chart 4 times; then repeat only Rnds 1–3 once. End the leg with 2 rnds in White. Break the working yarn in all colors.

Now work a boomerang heel in Tangerine in stockinette stitch over the 26 sts of Ndls 4 and 1, following instructions on page 179.

Work the foot in stockinette stitch in the round over all sts on all 4 DPNs, beginning with 2 rnds in White. Now continue in stranded pattern in White, Pastel Blue, and Tangerine. Work Rnds 1–6 of the chart 4 times, and then only Rnds 1–3 once. After this, work 2 rnds in White. Break the working yarn in White and Pastel Blue. Finish the sock in Tangerine, starting banded toe decreases after 4.7 in. / 12 cm from middle of heel.

Work toe with paired banded decreases according to instructions on page 185. Break the working yarn, and pull the end through to the inside of the sock.

Weave in all ends.

Work the second sock the same way.

Stockinette Stitch

In rows: Knit on RS, purl on WS.
In rnds: Knit all sts in all rnds.

Cuff Ribbing

Alternate "k1, p1."

Stranded Pattern

Stitch count has to be a multiple of 4.

Work all rnds in stockinette stitch according to the colorwork chart. Repeat the pattern repeat (4 sts wide) around.

Colorwork Chart

☐ = White
▨ = Pastel Blue
▧ = Tangerine

Pattern repeat = 4 stitches

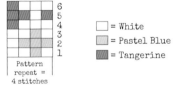

CHILD'S 1, foot length approximately 5 in./12.5 cm
CO 48 sts (12 sts per needle).
Leg, stranded pattern: Work Rnds 1-6 of chart twice; then work only Rnds 1-3 once.
Foot, stranded pattern: Work Rnds 1-6 of chart twice; then work only Rnds 1-3 once. Continue as stated in pattern, and after 3.75 in./9.5 cm from middle of heel, begin toe decreases.

CHILD'S 2-3, foot length approximately 5.5 in./14 cm
CO 48 sts (12 sts per needle).
Foot, stranded pattern: Work Rnds 1-6 of chart 3 times; then work only Rnds 1-3 once. Continue as stated in pattern, and after 4.3 in./11 cm from middle of heel, begin toe decreases.

CHILD'S 6-7, foot length approximately 6.5 in./16.5 cm
CO 52 sts (13 sts per needle).
Foot, stranded pattern: Work Rnds 1-6 of the chart 5 times; then work only Rnds 1-3 once. Continue as stated in pattern, and after 5.3 in./13.5 cm from middle of heel, begin toe decreases.

CHILD'S 8-10, foot length approximately 7.1 in./18 cm
CO 56 sts (14 sts per needle).
Leg, stranded pattern: Work Rnds 1-6 of the chart 5 times; then work only Rnds 1-3 once.
Foot, stranded pattern: Work Rnds 1-6 of the chart 5 times; then work only Rnds 1-3 once. Continue as stated in pattern, and after 5.5 in./14 cm from middle of heel, begin toe decreases.

SOXX 2

DIFFICULTY LEVEL 3

SIZES

Women's 5½–Men's 11

Pattern instructions as given are for Women's 7–8. Changes to stitch counts and variations needed for other sizes are given on page 17.

MATERIALS

Lang Yarns Jawoll, super fine (75% wool, 25% nylon; 230 yd./210 m; 1.75 oz./50 g), 1 skein each in #01 White, #159 Tangerine, and #220 Pastel Blue

DPNs, size US 1.5–2.5/2.5–3.0 mm

GAUGE

In colorwork pattern on US 1.5–2.5/2.5–3.0 mm needles, 38 sts and 40 rnds = 4 x 4 in./10 x 10 cm

INSTRUCTIONS

CO 64 sts in Pastel Blue, distribute evenly onto 4 DPNs (16 sts per needle), and join into the round.

For the cuff, work 13 rnds (1.2 in./3 cm) in Cuff Ribbing pattern.

Work the leg in stockinette stitch, beginning with 2 rnds in White; then continue in stranded pattern in White, Pastel Blue, and Tangerine. Work Rnds 1–7 of the chart 7 times; then break the working yarns.

Now work a boomerang heel in stockinette stitch in Pastel Blue over the 32 sts of Ndls 4 and 1, following instructions on page 179.

Work the foot in stockinette stitch in the round over all sts on all 4 DPNs, beginning with 2 rnds in White. Continue in stranded pattern in White, Pastel Blue, and Tangerine. Work Rnds 1–7 of the chart 7 times; then work 2 rnds in White. Break the working yarn in White and Tangerine. Finish the sock in Pastel Blue, starting banded toe decreases after 6.9 in./17.5 cm from middle of heel.

Work toe with paired banded decreases according to instructions on page 185. Break the working yarn, and pull the end through to the inside of the sock.

Weave in all ends.

Work the second sock the same way.

Stockinette Stitch
In rows: Knit on RS, purl on WS.
In rnds: Knit all sts in all rnds.

Cuff Ribbing
Alternate "k1, p1."

Stranded Pattern
Stitch count has to be a multiple of 4.
Work all rnds in stockinette stitch from the colorwork chart. Repeat the pattern repeat (4 sts wide) around.

Colorwork Chart

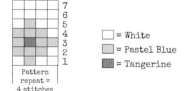

7
6
5
4
3
2
1

Pattern
repeat =
4 stitches

☐ = White
▨ = Pastel Blue
▧ = Tangerine

STITCH COUNTS AND VARIATIONS FOR OTHER SIZES

WOMEN'S 5½–6
CO 64 sts (16 sts per needle).
Foot, stranded pattern: Work Rnds 1–7 of chart 5 times.
Continue as stated in pattern, and after 6.3 in./16 cm from
middle of heel, begin toe decreases.

WOMEN'S 9–9½, MEN'S 7–7½
CO 68 sts (17 sts per needle).
Foot, stranded pattern: Work Rnds 1–7 of the chart 7 times.
Continue as stated in pattern, and after 7.5 in./19 cm from
middle of heel, begin toe decreases.

WOMEN'S 11–12, MEN'S 8½–9
CO 68 sts (17 sts per needle).
Foot, stranded pattern: Work Rnds 1–7 of chart 8 times.
Continue as stated in pattern, and after 8.1 in./20.5 cm from
middle of heel, begin toe decreases.

MEN'S 10–11
CO 72 sts (18 sts per needle).
Foot, stranded pattern: Work Rnds 1–7 of chart 8 times.
Continue as stated in pattern, and after 8.7 in./22 cm from
middle of heel, begin toe decreases.

SOXX 3

DIFFICULTY LEVEL 3

SIZES

Women's 9–Men's 13

Pattern instructions as given are for Women's 11–12 and Men's 8½–9. Changes to stitch counts and variations needed for other sizes are given on page 23.

MATERIALS

Lana Grossa Meilenweit 50, super fine (80% wool, 20% nylon; 230 yd./210 m; 1.75 oz./50 g), 1 skein each in #1362 Green, #1113 Nature, #1375 Light Blue, and #1363 Jeans

DPN set of 5 needles in size US 1.5–2.5/2.5–3.0 mm

GAUGE

In colorwork pattern on US 1.5–2.5/2.5–3.0 mm needles, 34 sts and 36 rnds = 4 x 4 in./10 x 10 cm

>Let's Have a Soxx Party<

Stockinette Stitch

In rows: Knit on RS, purl on WS.
In rnds: Knit all sts in all rnds.

Cuff Ribbing
Alternate "k2, p2."

Stranded Patterns A, B, and C

Stitch count has to be a multiple of 2 or 4.
Work all rnds in stockinette stitch from the
appropriate colorwork chart. Repeat the
pattern repeat (2 or 4 sts wide) around.

Stranded Pattern A

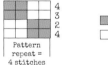

```
4
3
2
4
```
Pattern
repeat =
4 stitches

■ = Green
□ = Nature

Stranded Pattern B

```
2
1
```
Pattern
repeat =
2 stitches

□ = Nature
▨ = Light Blue

Stranded Pattern C

```
6
5
4
3
2
1
```
Pattern
repeat =
4 stitches

□ = Nature
■ = Jeans
▨ = Green
▨ = Light Blue

INSTRUCTIONS

CO 68 sts in Green, distribute evenly onto 4 DPNs (17 sts per needle), and join into the round.

For the cuff, work 14 rnds (1.2 in./3 cm) in Cuff Ribbing pattern.

Work the leg in stockinette stitch, beginning in stranded pattern from Chart A in Green and Nature. Work Rnds 1–4 of the chart twice. Now continue in Stranded Pattern B in Nature and Light Blue. Work Rnds 1 and 2 of the chart twice. Now continue in Stranded Pattern C in Nature, Jeans, Green, and Light Blue. Work Rnds 1–6 of the chart 5 times; then work only Rnds 1–5 once more. Now work 1 rnd in Nature, 2 rnds in Jeans, 1 rnd in Nature. Break the working yarn in all colors.

Work a boomerang heel in Light Blue in stockinette stitch over the 34 sts of Ndls 4 and 1, following the instructions on page 179.

Work the foot in stockinette stitch in the round over all sts on all 4 DPNs, beginning with 1 rnd in Nature, 2 rnds in Jeans, and 1 rnd in Nature. Then work in Stranded Pattern C in Nature, Jeans, Green, and Light Blue. Work Rnds 4–6 of the chart once; then Rnds 1–6, 5 times; then only Rnds 1 and 2 once more. Break the working yarn in Jeans. Now continue in Stranded Pattern B in Nature and Light Blue. Work Rnds 1 and 2 of the chart twice. Break the working yarn in Light Blue. Now continue in Stranded Pattern A in Green and Nature. Work Rnds 1–4 of the chart once. Break the working yarn in Nature, and finish the sock in Green. After 8.1 in./20.5 cm from middle of heel, begin toe decreases.

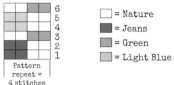

Work toe with paired banded decreases according to instructions on page 185. Break the working yarn, and pull the end through to the inside of the sock.

Weave in all ends.
Work the second sock the same way.

STITCH COUNTS AND VARIATIONS FOR OTHER SIZES

WOMEN'S 9–9½, MEN'S 7–7½
CO 68 sts (17 sts per needle).
Foot, Stranded Pattern C: Work Rnds 4–6 of the chart once; then work Rnds 1–6, 5 times, and only Rnds 1 and 2 once. Continue as stated in pattern, and after 7.5 in./19 cm from middle of heel, begin toe decreases.

MEN'S 10–11
CO 72 sts (18 sts per needle).
Foot, Stranded Pattern C: Work Rnds 4–6 of the chart once; then work Rnds 1–6, 7 times, and only Rnds 1 and 2 once. Continue as stated in pattern, and after 8.7 in./22 cm from middle of heel, begin toe decreases.

MEN'S 12–13
CO 76 sts (19 sts per needle).
Foot, Stranded Pattern C: Work Rnds 4–6 of the chart once; then work Rnds 1–6, 8 times, and only Rnds 1 and 2 once. Continue as stated in pattern, and after 9.3 in./23.5 cm from middle of heel, begin toe decreases.

SOXX 4

DIFFICULTY LEVEL 3

SIZES

Child's 11–Youth's 3

Pattern instructions as given are for Child's 11–12, foot length approximately 7.5 in./19 cm. Changes to stitch counts and variations needed for other sizes are given on page 28.

MATERIALS

Lana Grossa Meilenweit 50, super fine (80% wool, 20% nylon; 230 yd./210 m; 1.75 oz./50 g), 1 skein each in #1362 Green, #1101 White, #1283 Yellow, and #1372 Orange

DPN set of 5 needles in size US 1.5–2.5/2.5–3.0 mm

GAUGE

In colorwork pattern on US 1.5–2.5/2.5–3.0 mm needles, 32 sts and 38 rnds = 4 x 4 in./10 x 10 cm

Stockinette Stitch

In rows: Knit on RS, purl on WS.
In rnds: Knit all sts in all rnds.

Cuff Ribbing

Alternate "k1, p1."

Stranded Patterns A and B

Stitch count has to be a multiple of 4.
Work all rnds in stockinette stitch from the appropriate colorwork chart. Repeat the pattern repeat (4 sts wide) around.

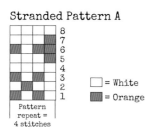

Stranded Pattern A

8
7
6
5
4
3
2
1

☐ = White
▨ = Orange

Pattern repeat = 4 stitches

Stranded Pattern B

7
6
5
4
3
2
1

☐ = White
▨ = Green

Pattern repeat = 4 stitches

INSTRUCTIONS

CO 56 sts in Yellow, distribute evenly onto 4 DPNs (14 sts per needle), and join into the round.

For the cuff, work 10 rnds (0.8 in./2 cm) in Cuff Ribbing pattern. Break the working yarn in Yellow.

Work the leg in stockinette stitch, beginning with 5 rnds in White. Now continue in Stranded Pattern A in White and Orange. Work Rnds 1–3 of the chart once. Then work 3 rnds in White. Now continue in Stranded Pattern B in White and Green. Work Rnds 1–7 of the chart once. Break the working yarn in Green, and work 3 rnds in White. Then continue in Stranded Pattern A in White and Orange. Work Rnds 1–8 of the chart twice; then work only Rnds 1–4 once more. Now work 1 more rnd in White. Break the working yarn in White and Orange.

Now work a boomerang heel in Yellow in stockinette stitch over the 28 sts of Ndls 4 and 1, following instructions on page 179.

Work the foot in stockinette stitch in the round over all sts on all 4 DPNs, beginning with 2 rnds in White. Then work Stranded Pattern A in White and Orange. Work Rnds 1–8 of the chart 4 times; then work only Rnds 1–4 once. Break the working yarn in Orange. Now work 1 rnd in White, 2 rnds in Green, and 2 rnds in White. Break the working yarn in White and Green, and finish the sock in Yellow. After 5.9 in./15 cm from middle of heel, begin toe decreases.

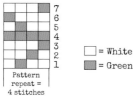

The leg for Child's 11-12 has a length of 5 in./12.5 cm and can be made longer or shorter by working a different number of repeats for Stranded Pattern A.

CHILD'S 6-7, foot length approximately 6.5 in./16.5 cm
CO 52 sts (13 sts per needle).
Foot, stranded pattern A: Work Rnds 1-8 of the chart 3 times; then only Rnds 1-4 once. Continue as stated in pattern, and after 5.3 in./13.5 cm from middle of heel, begin toe decreases.

CHILD'S 8-10, foot length approximately 7.1 in./18 cm
CO 56 sts (14 sts per needle).
Foot, stranded pattern A: Work Rnds 1-8 of the chart 4 times. Continue as stated in pattern, and after 5.5 in./14 cm from middle of heel, begin toe decreases.

CHILD'S 13, YOUTH'S 1, foot length approximately 8.1 in./20.5 cm
CO 60 sts (15 sts per needle).
Foot, stranded pattern A: Work Rnds 1-8 of the chart 5 times. Continue as stated in pattern, and after 6.5 in./16.5 cm from middle of heel, begin toe decreases.

YOUTH'S 2-3, foot length approximately 8.5 in./21.5 cm
CO 60 sts (15 sts per needle).
Foot, stranded pattern A: Work Rnds 1-8 of the chart 5 times; then work only Rnds 1-4 once. Continue as stated in pattern, and after 6.9 in./17.5 cm from middle of heel, begin toe decreases.

Work toe with paired banded decreases according to instructions on page 185. Break the working yarn, and pull the end through to the inside of the sock.

Weave in all ends.

Work the second sock the same way.

You're My Soxx,

You're My Soul >>>>

SOXX 5

DIFFICULTY LEVEL 3

SIZES

Women's 5½–Men's 11

Pattern instructions as given are for Women's 7–8. Changes to stitch counts and variations needed for other sizes are given on page 37.

MATERIALS

Lang Yarns Jawoll, super fine (75% wool, 25% nylon; 230 yd./210 m; 1.75 oz./50 g), 1 skein each in #94 Off-White, #159 Tangerine, #23 Light Grey Heathered, and #03 Dark Grey Heathered

DPN set of 5 needles in size US 1.5–2.5/2.5–3.0 mm

GAUGE

In colorwork pattern on US 1.5–2.5/2.5–3.0 mm needles, 36 sts and 40 rnds = 4 x 4 in./10 x 10 cm

Stockinette Stitch

In rows: Knit on RS, purl on WS.

In rnds: Knit all sts in all rnds.

Cuff Ribbing

Alternate "k1, p1."

Stranded Patterns A and B

Stitch count has to be a multiple of 4.

Work all rnds in stockinette stitch from the appropriate colorwork chart.

Repeat the pattern repeat (4 sts wide) around.

Stranded Pattern A

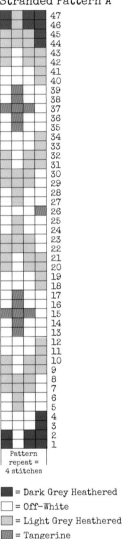

Pattern repeat = 4 stitches

■ = Dark Grey Heathered

☐ = Off-White

▨ = Light Grey Heathered

▨ = Tangerine

Stranded Pattern B

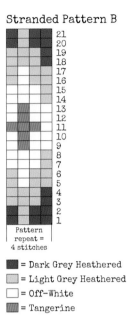

Pattern repeat = 4 stitches

■ = Dark Grey Heathered

▨ = Light Grey Heathered

☐ = Off-White

▨ = Tangerine

INSTRUCTIONS

CO 64 sts in Dark Grey Heathered, distribute evenly onto 4 DPNs (16 sts per needle), and join into the round.

For the cuff, work 13 rnds (1.2 in./3 cm) in Cuff Ribbing pattern.

Work the leg in stockinette stitch in Stranded Pattern A in Dark Grey Heathered, Off-White, Light Grey Heathered, and Tangerine. Work Rnds 1–47 of the chart once. After Rnd 4, break the working yarn in Dark Grey Heath- ered. In Rnd 44 of the chart, join this color anew, and break Tangerine and Off-White. Finish the leg with 7 Rnds in Dark Grey Heathered.

Now work a French heel in Dark Grey Heathered in stockinette stitch over the 32 sts of Ndls 4 and 1, following instructions on page 182.

Continue the foot in Dark Grey Heathered in stockinette stitch in the round over all sts on all 4 DPNs. After 3.5 in./9 cm from middle of heel, work Stranded Pattern B in Dark Grey Heathered, Light Grey Heathered, Off-White, and Tangerine. Work Rnds 1–21 of the chart once. Then break the working yarn in Light Grey Heathered, Tangerine, and Off-White, and finish the foot in Dark Grey Heathered. After 6.9 in./17.5 cm from middle of heel, begin toe decreases.

Work toe with paired banded decreases according to instructions on page 185. Break the working yarn, and pull the end through to the inside of the sock.

Weave in all ends.

Work the second sock the same way.

STITCH COUNTS AND VARIATIONS FOR OTHER SIZES

Please note that Stranded Pattern B starts only after the gusset decreases have been finished.

WOMEN'S 5½–6
CO 64 sts (16 sts per needle).
Foot: After 3.1 in./8 cm from middle of heel, begin Stranded Pattern B. After 6.3 in./16 cm from middle of heel, begin toe decreases.

WOMEN'S 9–9½, MEN'S 7–7½
CO 68 sts (17 sts per needle).
Foot: After 4 in./10 cm from middle of heel, begin Stranded Pattern B. After 7.5 in./19 cm from middle of heel, begin toe decreases.

WOMEN'S 11–12, MEN'S 8½–9
CO 68 sts (17 sts per needle).
Foot: After 4.3 in./11 cm from middle of heel, begin Stranded Pattern B. After 8.1 in./20.5 cm from middle of heel, begin toe decreases.

MEN'S 10–11
CO 72 sts (18 sts per needle).
Foot: After 4.7 in./12 cm from middle of heel, begin Stranded Pattern B. After 8.7 in./22 cm from middle of heel, begin toe decreases.

SOXX 6

SIZES

Women's 9–Men's 13

Pattern instructions as given are for Women's 11–12 and Men's 8½–9. Changes to stitch counts and variations needed for other sizes are given on page 41.

MATERIALS

Lana Grossa Meilenweit 50, super fine (80% wool, 20% nylon; 230 yd./210 m; 1.75 oz./50 g), 1 skein #1302 Pastel Blue Heathered and 2 skeins #1102 Beige-Grey Heathered

DPN set of 5 needles in size US 1.5–2.5/2.5–3.0 mm

GAUGE

In stockinette stitch on US 1.5–2.5/2.5–3.0 mm needles, 34 sts and 44 rnds = 4 x 4 in./10 x 10 cm

Stockinette Stitch

In rows: Knit on RS, purl on WS.

In rnds: Knit all sts in all rnds.

Knitting through the Back Loop (k-tbl)

Insert the needle from right to left into the back leg of the stitch; knit the stitch this way so it ends up twisted.

Cuff Ribbing

Alternate "k1-tbl, p1."

INSTRUCTIONS

CO 64 sts in Pastel Blue Heathered, distribute evenly onto 4 DPNs (16 sts per needle), and join into the round.

For the cuff, work 16 rnds Cuff Ribbing in Pastel Blue Heathered, followed by color sequence * 3 rnds Beige-Grey Heathered, 2 rnds Pastel Blue Heathered; rep from * twice (3.1 in./8 cm).

Work the leg in stockinette stitch. Continue the stripe pattern with * 3 rnds Beige-Grey Heathered, 2 rnds Pastel Blue Heathered; rep from * twice. Break the working yarn in Pastel Blue Heathered, and continue to the beginning of the heel, working 25 rnds in Beige-Grey Heathered.

Work a French heel in Beige-Grey Heathered over the 32 sts of Ndls 4 and 1, following instructions on page 182.

Work the foot in stockinette stitch in the round over all sts on all 4 DPNs, starting with 25 rnds in Beige-Grey Heathered. Then work * 2 rnds Pastel Blue Heathered, 3 rnds Beige-Grey Heathered; rep from * 6 times. Finish the stripe pattern with 2 rnds Pastel Blue Heathered. Break the working yarn in Pastel Blue Heathered, and finish the sock in Beige-Grey Heathered. After 8.1 in./20.5 cm from middle of heel, begin toe decreases.

Work toe with paired banded decreases according to instructions on page 185. Pull the tail through to the inside of the sock.

Weave in all ends.

Work the second sock the same way.

STITCH COUNTS AND VARIATIONS FOR OTHER SIZES

WOMEN'S 9–9½, MEN'S 7–7½
CO 64 sts (16 sts per needle).
Foot: Begin with 25 rnds in Beige-Grey Heathered. Then work
* 2 rnds Pastel Blue Heathered, 3 rnds Beige-Grey Heathered;
rep from * 5 times. Finish the stripe pattern with 2 rnds
Pastel Blue Heathered. After 7.5 in./19 cm from middle of
heel, begin toe decreases.

MEN'S 10–11
CO 68 sts (17 sts per needle).
Foot: Begin with 25 rnds in Beige-Grey Heathered. Then work
* 2 rnds Pastel Blue Heathered, 3 rnds Beige-Grey Heathered;
rep from * 7 times. Finish the stripe pattern with 2 rnds
Pastel Blue Heathered. After 8.7 in./22 cm from middle of
heel, begin toe decreases.

MEN'S 12–13
CO 72 sts (18 sts per needle).
Foot: Begin with 25 rnds in Beige-Grey Heathered. Then work
* 2 rnds Pastel Blue Heathered, 3 rnds Beige-Grey Heathered;
rep from * 8 times. Finish the stripe pattern with 2 rnds
Pastel Blue Heathered. After 9.3 in./23.5 cm from middle of
heel, begin toe decreases.

SOXX 7

DIFFICULTY LEVEL 3

SIZES

Women's 5½–Men's 11

Pattern instructions as given are for Women's 7–8. Changes to stitch counts and variations needed for other sizes are given on page 47.

MATERIALS

Lang Yarns Jawoll, super fine (75% wool, 25% nylon; 230 yd./210 m; 1.75 oz./50 g), 1 skein each in #94 Off-White, #248 Dusty Pink, #05 Grey Heathered, and #150 Gold

DPN set of 5 needles in size US 1.5–2.5/2.5–3.0 mm

GAUGE

In colorwork pattern on US 1.5–2.5/2.5–3.0 mm needles, 36 sts and 42 rnds = 4 x 4 in./10 x 10 cm

Stranded Patterns A and B

Stitch count has to be a multiple of 4.

Work all rnds in stockinette stitch from the appropriate colorwork chart. Repeat the pattern repeat (4 sts wide) around.

Stockinette Stitch

In rows: Knit on RS, purl on WS.
In rnds: Knit all sts in all rnds.

Cuff Ribbing

Alternate "k2, p2."

Stranded Pattern A

Pattern repeat = 4 stitches

▨ = Gold
☐ = Off-White

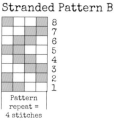

Stranded Pattern B

Pattern repeat = 4 stitches

☐ = Off-White
▨ = Dusty Pink

INSTRUCTIONS

CO 64 sts in Grey Heathered, distribute evenly onto 4 DPNs (16 sts per needle), and join into the round.

For the cuff, work 16 rnds (1.4 in./3.5 cm) in Cuff Ribbing pattern. Break the working yarn in Grey Heathered.

Work the leg in stockinette stitch, beginning with 2 rnds in Off-White. Continue in Stranded Pattern A in Gold and Off-White. Work Rnds 1–4 of the chart twice and then only Rnds 1 and 2 once. Break the working

yarn in Gold. Now work 2 rnds in Off-White, 2 rnds in Grey Heathered, and 2 rnds in Off-White. Break the working yarn in Grey Heathered. Then continue in Stranded Pattern B in Off-White and Dusty Pink. Work Rnds 1–8 of the chart 4 times; then work only Rnd 1 once more. Break the working yarn in Dusty Pink, and finish the leg with 2 rnds Off-White, 2 rnds Grey Heathered, and 2 rnds Off-White. Break the working yarn in both colors.

Now work a boomerang heel in Grey Heathered in stockinette stitch over the 32 sts of Ndls 4 and 1, following instructions on page 179. Work the foot in stockinette stitch in the round over all sts on all 4 DPNs, beginning with 2 rnds Off-White, 2 rnds Grey Heathered, and 2 rnds Off-White. Break the working yarn in Grey Heathered. Now continue in Stranded Pattern B in Off-White and Dusty Pink. Work Rnds 1–8 of the chart 4 times; then work only Rnd 1 once more. Break the working

yarn in Dusty Pink. Now work 2 rnds in Off-White, 2 rnds in Grey Heathered, and 2 rnds in Off-White. Continue in Stranded Pattern A in Gold and Off-White.

Work Rnds 1–4 of the chart once and then only Rnds 1 and 2 once. Then work 2 rnds in Off-White, and break the working yarn in Gold and Off-White. Finish the sock in Grey Heathered. After 8 in./20 cm from middle of heel, start decreases for the rounded toe.

Work rounded toe according to instructions on page 185. Graft the remaining opening in Kitchener stitch (see page 186).

Weave in all ends.

Work the second sock the same way.

WOMEN'S 5½–6
CO 64 sts (16 sts per needle).
Foot, Stranded Pattern B: Work Rnds 1–8 of the chart 3 times and then only Rnd 1 once. Stranded Pattern A: Work Rnds 1–4 of the chart once and then only Rnds 1 and 2 once. Continue as stated in pattern, and after 7.3 in./18.5 cm from middle of heel, start decreases for the rounded toe.

WOMEN'S 9–9½, MEN'S 7–7½
CO 68 sts (17 sts per needle).
Foot, Stranded Pattern B: Work Rnds 1–8 of the chart 4 times and then only Rnd 1 once. Stranded Pattern A: Work Rnds 1–4 of the chart twice and then only Rnds 1 and 2 once. Continue as stated in pattern, starting decreases for the rounded toe after 8.5 in./21.5 cm from middle of heel.

WOMEN'S 11–12, MEN'S 8½–9
CO 68 sts (17 sts per needle).
Foot, Stranded Pattern B: Work Rnds 1–8 of the chart 5 times and then only Rnd 1 once. Stranded Pattern A: Work Rnds 1–4 of the chart once and then only Rnds 1 and 2 once. Continue as stated in pattern, starting decreases for the rounded toe after 9.1 in./23 cm from middle of heel.

MEN'S 10–11
CO 72 sts (18 sts per needle).
Foot, Stranded Pattern B: Work Rnds 1–8 of the chart 5 times and then only Rnd 1 once. Stranded Pattern A: Work Rnds 1–4 of the chart once and then only Rnds 1 and 2 once. Continue as stated in pattern, starting decreases for the rounded toe after 9.6 in./24.5 cm from middle of heel.

SOXX 8

DIFFICULTY LEVEL 3

SIZES

Women's 5½–Men's 11

Pattern instructions as given are for Women's 7–8. Changes to stitch counts and variations needed for other sizes are given on page 52.

MATERIALS

Lang Yarns Jawoll, super fine (75% wool, 25% nylon; 230 yd./210 m; 1.75 oz./50 g), 1 skein each in #03 Dark Grey Heathered, #94 Off-White, and #248 Dusty Pink

DPN set of 5 needles in size US 1.5–2.5/2.5–3.0 mm

GAUGE

In colorwork pattern on US 1.5–2.5/2.5–3.0 mm needles, 36 sts and 42 rnds = 4 x 4 in./10 x 10 cm

Stockinette Stitch

In rows: Knit on RS, purl on WS.
In rnds: Knit all sts in all rnds.

Cuff Ribbing

Alternate "k1, p1."

Stranded Patterns A, B, C, D, and E

Stitch count has to be a multiple of either 2 or 4.
Work all rnds in stockinette stitch from the
appropriate colorwork chart. Repeat the
pattern repeat (2 or 4 sts wide) around.

Stranded Pattern A

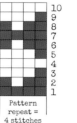

= Dark Grey Heathered
= Off–White

Pattern
repeat =
4 stitches

Stranded Pattern B

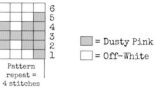

= Dusty Pink
= Off–White

Pattern
repeat =
4 stitches

Stranded Pattern C

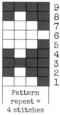

= Dusty Pink
= Off–White

Pattern
repeat =
2 stitches

Stranded Pattern D

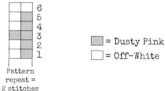

= Dark Grey Heathered
= Off–White

Pattern
repeat =
4 stitches

Stranded Pattern E

= Dark Grey Heathered
= Off–White

Pattern
repeat =
2 stitches

INSTRUCTIONS

CO 64 sts in Dark Grey Heathered, distribute evenly onto 4 DPNs (16 sts per needle), and join into the round.

For the cuff, work 12 rnds (1 in./2.5 cm) in Dark Grey Heathered in Cuff Ribbing.

Work the leg in stockinette stitch, beginning with Stranded Pattern A in Dark Grey Heathered and Off-White. Work Rnds 1–10 of the chart once. Break the working yarn in Dark Grey Heathered. Now continue in Stranded Pattern B in Dusty Pink and Off-White. Work Rnds 1–6 of chart 8 times. Break the working yarn in Off-White and Dusty Pink.

Now work a French heel in Dark Grey Heathered in stockinette stitch over the 32 sts of Ndls 4 and 1, following instructions on page 182. Then pick up and knit sts from the edges of the heel flap according to Stranded Pattern C in Dusty Pink and Off-White, working the last stitch of Ndl 1 and the first stitch of Ndl 4 in Stranded Pattern B.

Work the foot in stockinette stitch in the round over all sts on all 4 DPNs. Work the instep (Ndls 2 and 3) in Stranded Pattern B in Dusty Pink and Off-White. Work Rnds 1–6 of the chart 5 times. At the same time, work the sole (Ndls 4 and 1) in Stranded Pattern C.

Work Rnds 1–6 of the chart 5 times. For a neater-looking transition between the sole and the instep, work the last stitch of Ndl 1 and the first stitch of Ndl 4 in Stranded Pattern B. Break the working yarn in Dusty Pink. Now continue the instep in Stranded Pattern D in Dark Grey Heathered and Off-White. Work Rnds 1–9 of the chart once. At the same time, work the sole in Stranded Pattern E in Dark Grey Heathered and Off-White. Work Rnds 1–6 of the chart once; then repeat only Rnds 1–3 once.

Break the working yarn in Off-White, and finish the sock in Dark Grey Heathered. After 6.9 in./17.5 cm from middle of heel, begin toe decreases.

Work toe with paired banded decreases according to instructions on page 185. Break the working yarn, and pull the end through to the inside of the sock.

Weave in all ends.

Work the second sock the same way.

STITCH COUNTS AND VARIATIONS FOR OTHER SIZES

WOMEN'S 5½–6
CO 64 sts (16 sts per needle).
Foot, Stranded Patterns B and C: Work Rnds 1–6 of the chart 5 times. Continue as stated in pattern, and after 6.3 in./16 cm from middle of heel, begin toe decreases.

WOMEN'S 9–9½, MEN'S 7–7½
CO 68 sts (17 sts per needle).
Foot, Stranded Patterns B and C: Work Rnds 1–6 of the chart 7 times. Continue as stated in pattern, and after 7.5 in./19 cm from middle of heel, begin toe decreases.

WOMEN'S 11–12, MEN'S 8½–9
CO 68 sts (17 sts per needle).
Foot, Stranded Patterns B and C: Work Rnds 1–6 of the chart 8 times. Continue as stated in pattern, and after 8.1 in./20.5 cm from middle of heel, begin toe decreases.

MEN'S 10–11
CO 72 sts (18 sts per needle).
Foot, Stranded Patterns B and C: Work Rnds 1–6 of the chart 9 times. Continue as stated in pattern, and after 8.7 in./22 cm from middle of heel, begin toe decreases.

soxx 9

DIFFICULTY LEVEL 3

SIZES

Women's 9–Men's 13

Pattern instructions as given are for Women's 11–12 and Men's 8½–9. Changes to stitch counts and variations needed for other sizes are given on page 59.

MATERIALS

Lang Yarns Jawoll, super fine (75% wool, 25% nylon; 230 yd./210 m; 1.75 oz./50 g), 1 skein each in #70 Anthracite Heathered, #23 Light Grey Heathered, and #339 Camel

DPN set of 5 needles in size US 1.5–2.5/2.5–3.0 mm

GAUGE

In colorwork pattern on US 1.5–2.5/2.5–3.0 mm needles, 38 sts and 38 rnds = 4 x 4 in./10 x 10 cm

Stockinette Stitch

In rows: Knit on RS, purl on WS.

In rnds: Knit all sts in all rnds.

Cuff Ribbing

Alternate "k2, p2."

Stranded Patterns A, B, C, D, E, and F

Stitch count has to be a multiple of 4.

Work all rnds in stockinette stitch from the appropriate colorwork chart. Repeat the pattern repeat (4 sts wide) around.

SOCK 1

Stranded Pattern A

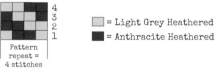

⬜ = Light Grey Heathered
⬛ = Anthracite Heathered

Stranded Pattern B

⬛ = Anthracite Heathered
⬜ = Light Grey Heathered

Stranded Pattern C

⬛ = Anthracite Heathered
🟫 = Camel

SOCK 2

Stranded Pattern D

⬛ = Anthracite Heathered
⬜ = Light Grey Heathered

Stranded Pattern E

⬛ = Anthracite Heathered
⬜ = Light Grey Heathered

Stranded Pattern F

⬛ = Anthracite Heathered
🟫 = Camel

INSTRUCTIONS

CO 68 sts in Anthracite Heathered, distribute evenly onto 4 DPNs (17 sts per needle), and join into the round.

For the cuff, work in Cuff Ribbing pattern, first 10 rnds in Anthracite Heathered and then 3 rnds "k2 in Anthracite Heathered, p2 in Camel" (1.2 in./3 cm).

Work the leg in stockinette stitch, beginning with 3 rnds "k2 in Anthracite Heathered, k2 in Camel." Break the working yarn in Camel.

SOCK 1: Continue in Stranded Pattern A in Light Grey Heathered and Anthracite Heathered. Work Rnds 1–4 of the chart 11 times. Break the working yarn in both colors.

SOCK 2: Continue in Stranded Pattern D in Anthracite Heathered and Light Grey Heath-ered. Work Rnds 1–4 of the chart 11 times. Break the working yarn in both colors.

Now work a boomerang heel in stockinette stitch in Camel over the 34 sts of Ndls 4 and 1, following instructions on page 179.

Work the foot in stockinette stitch in the round over all sts on all 4 DPNs, beginning with 2 rnds in Camel. Break the working yarn.

SOCK 1: Now continue in Stranded Pattern B in Anthracite Heathered and Light Grey Heath-ered. Work Rnds 1–4, 12 times. Break the working yarn in Light Grey Heathered. Now continue in Stranded Pattern C in Anthracite Heathered and Camel. Work Rnds 1–4 of the chart once. Break the working yarn in Anthra-cite Heathered, and finish the sock in Camel.

SOCK 2: Now continue in Stranded Pattern E in Anthracite Heathered and Light Grey Heathered. Work Rnds 1–4, 12 times. Break the working yarn in Light Grey Heathered. Continue in Stranded Pattern F in Anthracite Heathered and Camel. Work Rnds 1–4 of the chart once. Break the working yarn in Anthracite Heathered, and finish the sock in Camel.

After 8.1 in./20.5 cm from middle of heel, begin toe decreases.

Work toe with paired banded decreases according to instructions on page 185. Break the working yarn, and pull the end through to the inside of the sock.

Weave in all ends.

STITCH COUNTS AND VARIATIONS FOR OTHER SIZES

WOMEN'S 9–9$\frac{1}{2}$, MEN'S 7–7$\frac{1}{2}$
CO 68 sts (17 sts per needle).
Foot, Stranded Pattern B (Sock 1) or E (Sock 2): Work Rnds 1–4 of the appropriate chart 10 times. Continue as stated in pattern, and after 7.5 in./19 cm from middle of heel, begin toe decreases.

MEN'S 10–11
CO 72 sts (18 sts per needle).
Foot, Stranded Pattern B (Sock 1) or E (Sock 2): Work Rnds 1–4 of the appropriate chart 13 times. Continue as stated in pattern, and after 8.7 in./22 cm from middle of heel, begin toe decreases.

MEN'S 12–13
CO 76 sts (19 sts per needle).
Foot, Stranded Pattern B (Sock 1) or E (Sock 2): Work Rnds 1–4 of the appropriate chart 14 times. Continue as stated in pattern, and after 9.3 in./23.5 cm from middle of heel, begin toe decreases.

SOXX 10

DIFFICULTY LEVEL 3

SIZES

Women's 5½–Men's 11

Pattern instructions as given are for Women's 7–8. Changes to stitch counts and variations needed for other sizes are given on page 63.

MATERIALS

Schachenmayr Regia 4-Ply, super fine (75% wool, 25% polyam-ide; 230 yd./210 m; 1.75 oz./50 g), 1 skein each in #6618 Pink Lady, #2080 SuperWhite, and #33 Flannel Streaked

DPN set of 5 needles in size US 1.5–2.5/2.5–3.0 mm

GAUGE

In colorwork pattern on US 1.5–2.5/2.5–3.0 mm needles, 34 sts and 38 rnds = 4 x 4 in./10 x 10 cm

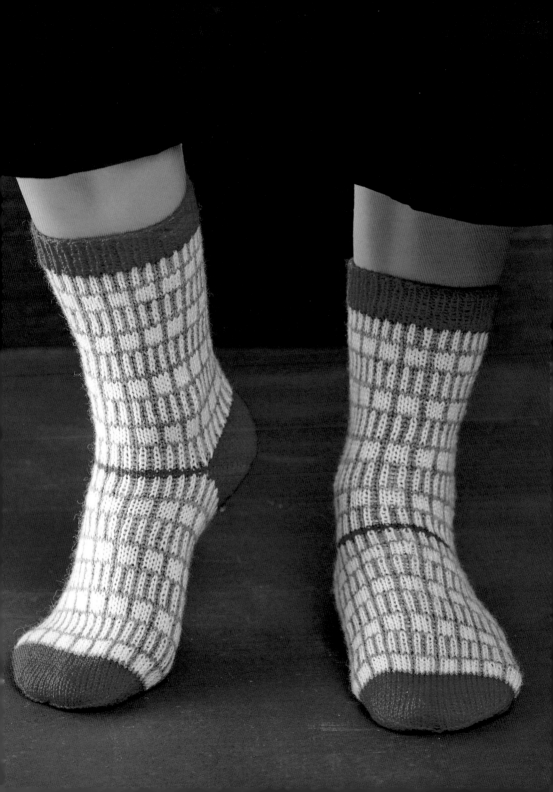

INSTRUCTIONS

CO 64 sts in Pink Lady, distribute evenly onto 4 DPNs (16 sts per needle), and join into the round.

For the cuff, work 12 rnds (1 in./2.5 cm) in Cuff Ribbing pattern; then break the working yarn.

Work the leg in stockinette stitch in stranded pattern in Flannel Streaked and SuperWhite. Work Rnds 1–11 of the chart 4 times; then work only Rnds 1–5 once more. Break the working yarn in both colors.

Now work a boomerang heel in Pink Lady in stockinette stitch over the 32 sts of Ndls 4 and 1, following instructions on page 179.

Work the foot in stockinette stitch in the round over all sts on all 4 DPNs. Continue in stranded pattern in Flannel Streaked and SuperWhite. Work Rnds 1–11 of the chart 4 times. Break the working yarn in both colors. Finish the sock in Pink Lady, beginning toe decreases after 6.9 in./17.5 cm from middle of heel.

Work toe with paired banded decreases according to instructions on page 185. Break the working yarn, and pull the end through to the inside of the sock.

Weave in all ends.

Work the second sock the same way.

Stockinette Stitch

In rows: Knit on RS, purl on WS.

In rnds: Knit all sts in all rnds.

Cuff Ribbing

Alternate "k1, p1."

Stranded Pattern

Stitch count has to be a multiple of 4.

Work all rnds in stockinette stitch according to the colorwork chart. Repeat the pattern repeat (4 sts wide) around.

Colorwork Chart

☒ = Flannel Streaked
☐ = SuperWhite

STITCH COUNTS AND VARIATIONS FOR OTHER SIZES

WOMEN'S 5½–6
CO 64 sts (16 sts per needle).
Foot, stranded pattern: Work Rnds 1–11 of the chart 3 times and then only Rnds 1–6 once. After 6.3 in./16 cm from middle of heel, begin toe decreases.

WOMEN'S 9–9½, MEN'S 7–7½
CO 68 sts (17 sts per needle).
Foot, stranded pattern: Work Rnds 1–11 of the chart 4 times and then only Rnds 1–6 once. After 7.5 in./19 cm from middle of heel, begin toe decreases.

WOMEN'S 11–12, MEN'S 8½–9
CO 68 sts (17 sts per needle).
Foot, stranded pattern: Work Rnds 1–11 of the chart 5 times. After 8.1 in./20.5 cm from middle of heel, begin toe decreases.

MEN'S 10–11
CO 72 sts (18 sts per needle).
Foot, stranded pattern: Work Rnds 1–11 of the chart 5 times; then only Rnds 1–6 once. After 8.7 in./22 cm from middle of heel, begin toe decreases.

I'm Sailing

in My Soxx »»»»»»

SOXX II

DIFFICULTY LEVEL 3

SIZES

Women's 5½–Men's 11

Pattern instructions as given are for Women's 7–8. Changes to stitch counts and variations needed for other sizes are given on page 70.

MATERIALS

Schachenmayr Regia 4-Ply, super fine (75% wool, 25% polyamide; 230 yd./210 m; 1.75 oz./50 g), 1 skein each in #2080 SuperWhite, #324 Marine, #17 Light Camel Heathered, and #2002 Cherry

DPN set of 5 needles in size US 1.5–2.5/2.5–3.0 mm

GAUGE

In colorwork pattern on US 1.5–2.5/2.5–3.0 mm needles, 34 sts and 38 rnds = 4 x 4 in./10 x 10 cm

Stockinette Stitch

In rows: Knit on RS, purl on WS.
In rnds: Knit all sts in all rnds.

Knitting through the Back Loop (k-tbl)

Insert the needle from right to left into the back
leg of the stitch; knit the stitch this way so it
ends up twisted.

Cuff Ribbing

Alternate "k1-tbl, p1."

Stranded Patterns A and B

Stitch count has to be a multiple of 4.
Work all rnds in stockinette stitch from the
appropriate colorwork chart. Repeat the
pattern repeat (4 sts wide) around.

Stranded Pattern A

Pattern
repeat =
4 stitches

☐ = SuperWhite
■ = Cherry

Stranded Pattern B

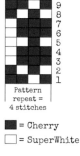

Pattern
repeat =
4 stitches

■ = Cherry
☐ = SuperWhite

INSTRUCTIONS

CO 64 sts in Marine, distribute evenly onto 4
DPNs (16 sts per needle), and join into the
round.

For the cuff, work 12 rnds (1.2 in./3 cm) in Cuff
Ribbing pattern; then break the working
yarn.

Work the leg in stockinette stitch, beginning
with 2 rnds in SuperWhite. Continue in
Stranded Pattern A in SuperWhite and
Cherry. Work Rnds 1–12 of the chart 3 times;
then work Rnds 13–15 once. Now work 2
rnds SuperWhite, 2 rnds Light Camel Heathered, 2 rnds SuperWhite, 2 rnds Cherry, and 2
rnds SuperWhite. Break the working yarn in
all colors.

Work a boomerang heel in Light Camel Heathered in stockinette stitch over the 32 sts of
Ndls 4 and 1, following instructions on page
179.

Work the foot in stockinette stitch in the round
over all sts on all 4 DPNs, beginning with 2
rnds SuperWhite, 2 rnds Cherry, 2 rnds
SuperWhite, 2 rnds Light Camel Heathered, 2
rnds SuperWhite, and 2 rnds Cherry. Break
the working yarn in Light Camel Heathered.
Now continue in Stranded Pattern B in
Cherry and SuperWhite. Work Rnds 1 and 2
of the chart once; then work Rnds 3–5, 8
times, and then Rnds 6–9 once. Continue
with 2 rnds Cherry, and break both working
yarns. Finish the sock in Marine. After 6.9
in./17.5 cm from middle of heel, begin toe
decreases.

Work toe with paired banded decreases according to instructions on page 185. Break the working yarn, and pull the end through to the inside of the sock.

Weave in all ends.
Work the second sock the same way.

STITCH COUNTS AND VARIATIONS FOR OTHER SIZES

WOMEN'S 5½–6
CO 64 sts (16 sts per needle).
Foot, Stranded Pattern B: Work Rnds 1 and 2 of the chart once, Rnds 3–5, 5 times, and then Rnds 6–9 once. Continue as stated in pattern, and after 6.3 in./16 cm from middle of heel, begin toe decreases.

WOMEN'S 9–9½, MEN'S 7–7½
CO 68 sts (17 sts per needle).
Foot, Stranded Pattern B: Work Rnds 1 and 2 of the chart once, Rnds 3–5, 10 times, and then Rnds 6–9 once. Continue as stated in pattern, and after 7.5 in./19 cm from middle of heel, begin toe decreases.

WOMEN'S 11–12, MEN'S 8½–9
CO 68 sts (17 sts per needle).
Foot, Stranded Pattern B: Work Rnds 1 and 2 of the chart once, Rnds 3–5, 12 times, and then Rnds 6–9 once. Continue as stated in pattern, and after 8.1 in./20.5 cm from middle of heel, begin toe decreases.

MEN'S 10–11
CO 72 sts (18 sts per needle).
Foot, Stranded Pattern B: Work Rnds 1 and 2 of the chart once, Rnds 3–5, 13 times, and then Rnds 6–9 once. Continue as stated in pattern, and after 8.7 in./22 cm from middle of heel, begin toe decreases.

SOXX 12

DIFFICULTY LEVEL 1

SIZES

Child's 6–Youth's 3

Pattern instructions as given are for Child's 11–12, foot length approximately 7.5 in./19 cm. Changes to stitch counts and variations needed for other sizes are given on page 75.

MATERIALS

Schachenmayr Regia 4-Ply, super fine (75% wool, 25% polyamide; 230 yd./210 m; 1.75 oz./50 g), 1 skein each in #2080 SuperWhite, #324 Marine, and #2002 Cherry

DPN set of 5 needles in size US 1.5–2.5/2.5–3.0 mm

GAUGE

In stockinette stitch on US 1.5–2.5/2.5–3.0 mm needles, 32 sts and 44 rnds = 4 x 4 in./10 x 10 cm

Stockinette Stitch

In rows: Knit on RS, purl on WS.
In rnds: Knit all sts in all rnds.

Knitting through the Back Loop (k-tbl)

Insert the needle from right to left into the back leg of the stitch; knit the stitch this way so it ends up twisted.

Cuff Ribbing

Alternate "k1-tbl, p1."

Stripe Pattern

Work all rnds in stockinette stitch from the colorwork chart. Repeat the pattern repeat (4 sts wide) around.

INSTRUCTIONS

CO 52 sts in Marine, distribute evenly onto 4 DPNs (13 sts per needle), and join into the round.

For the cuff, work 15 rnds (1.6 in./4 cm) in Cuff Ribbing pattern.

Work the leg in stockinette stitch in stripe sequence, working Rnds 1–14 of the chart 3 times in all. Then work 2 more rnds in Marine. Break the working yarn in Super-White and Cherry.

Now work a French heel in stockinette stitch in Marine over the 26 sts of Ndls 4 and 1, following instructions on page 182.

Continue the foot in Marine in stockinette stitch in the round over all sts on all 4 DPNs. After 5.3 in./13.5 cm from middle of heel, work * 2 rnds SuperWhite, 2 rnds Marine; rep from * once, beginning toe decreases after 5.9 in./15 cm from middle of heel. Break the working yarn in Marine and SuperWhite, and finish the sock in Cherry.

Work toe with paired banded decreases according to instructions on page 185. Break the working yarn, and pull the end through to the inside of the sock.

Weave in all ends.

Work the second sock the same way.

Colorwork Chart

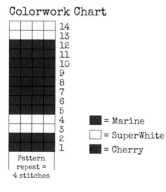

14
13
12
11
10
9
8
7
6
5
4
3
2
1

■ = Marine
□ = SuperWhite
■ = Cherry

Pattern repeat = 4 stitches

STITCH COUNTS AND VARIATIONS FOR OTHER SIZES

CHILD'S 6–7, foot length approximately 6.5 in./16.5 cm
CO 48 sts (12 sts per needle).
Leg: Work Rnds 1–14 of the chart twice.
Foot: After 4.7 in./12 cm from middle of heel, start stripe sequence according to instructions, and after 5.3 in./13.5 cm from middle of heel, begin toe decreases.

CHILD'S 8–10, foot length approximately 7.1 in./18 cm
CO 52 sts (13 sts per needle).
Foot: After 5 in./12.5 cm from middle of heel, start stripe sequence according to instructions, and after 5.5 in./14 cm from middle of heel, begin toe decreases.

CHILD'S 13, YOUTH'S 1, foot length approximately 8.1 in./20.5 cm
CO 56 sts (14 sts per needle).
Foot: After 5.9 in./15 cm from middle of heel, start stripe sequence according to instructions, and after 6.5 in./16.5 cm from middle of heel, begin toe decreases.

YOUTH'S 2–3, foot length approximately 8.5 in./21.5 cm
CO 56 sts (14 sts per needle).
Foot: After 6.3 in./16 cm from middle of heel, start stripe sequence according to instructions, and after 6.9 in./17.5 cm from middle of heel, begin toe decreases.

SOXX 13

DIFFICULTY LEVEL 2

SIZES

Women's 5½–Men's 11

Pattern instructions as given are for Women's 7–8.
Changes to stitch counts and variations needed for
other sizes are given on page 78.

MATERIALS

Schachenmayr Regia 4-Ply, super fine (75% wool, 25%
polyamide; 230 yd./210 m; 1.75 oz./50 g), 1 skein each
in #522 Anthracite Heathered, #2080 SuperWhite, and
#2002 Cherry

DPN set of 5 needles in size US 1.5–2.5/2.5–3.0 mm

GAUGE

In colorwork pattern on US 1.5–2.5/2.5–3.0 mm needles,
34 sts and 38 rnds = 4 x 4 in./10 x 10 cm

WOMEN'S 5½–6
CO 60 sts (15 sts per needle).
Foot: After 6.3 in./16 cm from middle of heel, begin toe decreases.

WOMEN'S 9–9½, MEN'S 7–7½
CO 64 sts (16 sts per needle).
Foot: After 7.5 in./19 cm from middle of heel, begin toe decreases.

WOMEN'S 11–12, MEN'S 8½–9
CO 64 sts (16 sts per needle).
Foot: Begin stranded pattern after 5.5 in./14 cm from middle of heel; work Rnds 1–9 of the chart once. Continue as stated in pattern, and after 8.1 in./20.5 cm from middle of heel, begin toe decreases.

MEN'S 10–11
CO 68 sts (17 sts per needle).
Foot: Begin stranded pattern after 6.1 in./15.5 cm from middle of heel; work Rnds 1–9 of the chart once. Continue as stated in pattern, and after 8.7 in./22 cm from middle of heel, begin toe decreases.

Stockinette Stitch

In rows: Knit on RS, purl on WS.
In rnds: Knit all sts in all rnds.

Cuff Ribbing

Alternate "k2, p2."

Stranded Pattern

Stitch count has to be a multiple of 4.
Work all rnds in stockinette stitch according to the colorwork chart. Repeat the pattern repeat (4 sts wide) around.

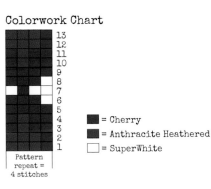

Colorwork Chart

Pattern repeat = 4 stitches

= Cherry
= Anthracite Heathered
= SuperWhite

INSTRUCTIONS

CO 60 sts in Anthracite Heathered, distribute evenly onto 4 DPNs (15 sts per needle), and join into the round.
For the cuff, work 16 rnds (1.4 in./3.5 cm) in Cuff Ribbing pattern.

Begin the leg with 5 rnds in Anthracite Heathered; then continue in stranded pattern in Cherry, Anthracite Heathered, and SuperWhite. Work Rnds 1–13 of the chart once. Then work 5 rnds in Anthracite Heathered. Continue in stranded pattern from colorwork chart. Work Rnds 1–13 of the chart once; then break the working yarn in Cherry and SuperWhite, and work 10 rnds in Anthracite Heathered.

Now work a French heel in Anthracite Heathered in stockinette stitch over the 30 sts of Ndls 4 and 1, following instructions on page 182.

Continue the foot in Anthracite Heathered in stockinette stitch in the round over all sts on all 4 DPNs. After 4.3 in./11 cm from middle of heel, continue in stranded pattern in Cherry, Anthracite Heathered, and SuperWhite. Work Rnds 1–9 of the chart once. Break the working yarn in Anthracite Heathered and SuperWhite, and finish the sock in Cherry. After 6.9 in./17.5 cm from middle of heel, begin toe decreases.

Work toe with paired banded decreases according to instructions on page 185. Break the working yarn, and pull the end through to the inside of the sock.

Weave in all ends.

Work the second sock the same way.

SOXX 14

DIFFICULTY LEVEL 3

SIZES

Women's 5½–Men's 11

Pattern instructions as given are Women's 7–8. Changes to stitch counts and variations needed for other sizes are given on page 85.

MATERIALS

Lang Yarns Jawoll, super fine (75% wool, 25% nylon; 230 yd./210 m; 1.75 oz./50 g), 1 skein each in #61 Burgundy, #226 Beige, #45 Light Brown Heathered, and #32 Jeans

DPN set of 5 needles in size US 1.5–2.5/2.5–3.0 mm

GAUGE

In colorwork pattern on US 1.5–2.5/2.5–3.0 mm needles, 34 sts and 40 rnds = 4 x 4 in./10 x 10 cm

> I'm Sailing in My Soxx <

Stockinette Stitch

In rows: Knit on RS, purl on WS.
In rnds: Knit all sts in all rnds.

Knitting through the Back Loop (k-tbl)

Insert the needle from right to left into the back
   leg of the stitch; knit the stitch this way so it
   ends up twisted.

Cuff Ribbing

Alternate "k1-tbl, p1."

Stranded Patterns A, B, C, and D

Stitch count has to be a multiple of 4.
Work all rnds in stockinette stitch from the
   appropriate colorwork chart. Repeat the
   pattern repeat (4 sts wide) around.

Stranded Pattern A

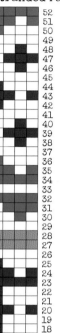

52
51
50
49
48
47
46
45
44
43
42
41
40
39
38
37
36
35
34
33
32
31
30
29
28
27
26
25
24
23
22
21
20
19
18
17
16
15
14
13
12
11
10
9
8
7
6
5
4
3
2
1

Pattern
repeat =
4 stitches

Stranded Pattern B

4
3
2
1

Pattern
repeat =
4 stitches

■ = Jeans
□ = Beige

Stranded Pattern C

5
4
3
2
1

Pattern
repeat =
4 stitches

□ = Beige
■ = Burgundy

Stranded Pattern D

10
9
8
7
6
5
4
3
2
1

Pattern
repeat =
4 stitches

□ = Beige
■ = Jeans
■ = Burgundy

▦ = Light Brown Heathered
□ = Beige
■ = Jeans
■ = Burgundy

INSTRUCTIONS

CO 64 sts in Burgundy, distribute evenly onto 4 DPNs (16 sts per needle), and join into the round.

For the cuff, work 15 rnds (1.4 in./3.5 cm) in Cuff Ribbing pattern.

Work the leg in stockinette stitch, beginning with 1 rnd in Burgundy; then continue in Stranded Pattern A in Light Brown Heathered, Beige, Jeans, and Burgundy. Work Rnds 1–52 of the chart once. Break the working yarn in Beige and Burgundy. Work 2 rnds in Light Brown Heathered and 2 rnds in Jeans.

Then break the working yarn in Jeans and Light Brown Heathered.

Now work a boomerang heel in Light Brown Heathered in stockinette stitch over the 32 sts of Ndls 4 and 1 according to instructions on page 179.

Work the foot in stockinette stitch in the round. Begin with 2 rnds in Jeans and 2 rnds in Light Brown Heathered. Break the working yarn in Light Brown Heathered. Then work Stranded Pattern B in Jeans and Beige. Work Rnds 1–4 of the chart once. Break the working yarn in

Jeans, and continue in Stranded Pattern C in Beige and Burgundy. Work Rnds 1–5 of the chart 4 times; then continue in Stranded Pattern D in Beige, Jeans, and Burgundy. Work Rnds 1–7 of the chart once; then work Rnds 1–10 once. Break the working yarn in Beige and Jeans, and finish the sock in Burgundy. After 6.9 in./17.5 cm from middle of heel, begin toe decreases.

Work toe with paired banded decreases according to instructions on page 185. Break the working yarn, and pull the end through to the inside of the sock.
Weave in all ends.
Work the second sock the same way.

STITCH COUNTS AND VARIATIONS FOR OTHER SIZES

WOMEN'S 5½-6
CO 64 sts (16 sts per needle).
Foot, Stranded Patterns B and D: Work according to instructions. Stranded Pattern C: Work Rnds 1-5 of the chart 3 times. Continue as stated in pattern, and after 6.3 in./16 cm from middle of heel, begin toe decreases.

WOMEN'S 9-9½, MEN'S 7-7½
CO 68 sts (17 sts per needle).
Foot, Stranded Patterns B and D: Work according to instructions. Stranded Pattern C: Work Rnds 1-5 of the chart 5 times. Continue as stated in pattern, and after 7.5 in./19 cm from middle of heel, begin toe decreases.

WOMEN'S 11-12, MEN'S 8½-9
CO 68 sts (17 sts per needle).
Foot, Stranded Patterns B and D: Work according to instructions. Stranded Pattern C: Work Rnds 1-5 of the chart 5 times. Continue as stated in pattern, and after 8.1 in./20.5 cm from middle of heel, begin toe decreases.

MEN'S 10-11
CO 72 sts (18 sts per needle).
Foot, Stranded Patterns B and D: Work according to instructions. Stranded Pattern C: Work Rnds 1-5 of the chart 7 times. Continue as stated in pattern, and after 8.7 in./22 cm from middle of heel, begin toe decreases.

SOXX 15

DIFFICULTY LEVEL 3

SIZES

Women's 5½–Men's 9

Pattern instructions as given are for Women's 7–8.
Changes to stitch counts and variations needed for other
sizes are given on page 92.

MATERIALS

Schachenmayr Regia 4-Ply, super fine (75% wool, 25%
polyamide; 230 yd./210 m; 1.75 oz./50 g), 1 skein each in
#2080 SuperWhite, #1945 Light Blue, and #2002 Cherry

DPN set of 5 needles in size US 1.5–2.5/2.5–3.0 mm

GAUGE

In colorwork pattern on US 1.5–2.5/2.5–3.0 mm needles,
32 sts and 40 rnds = 4 x 4 in./10 x 10 cm

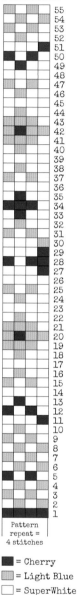

55
54
53
52
51
50
49
48
47
46
45
44
43
42
41
40
39
38
37
36
35
34
33
32
31
30
29
28
27
26
25
24
23
22
21
20
19
18
17
16
15
14
13
12
11
10
9
8
7
6
5
4
3
2
1

Pattern
repeat =
4 stitches

■ = Cherry
▨ = Light Blue
☐ = SuperWhite

Stockinette Stitch

In rows: Knit on RS, purl on WS.
In rnds: Knit all sts in all rnds.

Cuff Ribbing

Alternate "k2, p2."

Stranded Patterns A, B, C, D, E, and F
(leg and instep)

Stitch count has to be a multiple of 4.
Work all rnds in stockinette stitch from the appropriate colorwork chart. Repeat the pattern repeat (4 sts wide) around.

Stranded Patterns SB, SC, SD, SE, and SF
(sole of the foot)

Stitch count has to be a multiple of 2.
Work all rnds in stockinette stitch from the appropriate colorwork chart. Repeat the pattern repeat (2 sts wide) around.

Stranded Pattern B

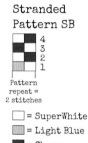

4
3
2
1

Pattern repeat = 4 stitches

☐ = SuperWhite
▨ = Light Blue
■ = Cherry

Stranded Pattern SB

4
3
2
1

Pattern repeat = 2 stitches

☐ = SuperWhite
▨ = Light Blue
■ = Cherry

Stranded Pattern C

3
2
1

Pattern repeat = 4 stitches

☐ = SuperWhite
▨ = Light Blue

Stranded Pattern SC

3
2
1

Pattern repeat = 2 stitches

☐ = SuperWhite
▨ = Light Blue

Stranded Pattern D

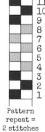

11
10
9
8
7
6
5
4
3
2
1

Pattern repeat = 4 stitches

☐ = SuperWhite
■ = Cherry
▨ = Light Blue

Stranded Pattern SD

11
10
9
8
7
6
5
4
3
2
1

Pattern repeat = 2 stitches

☐ = SuperWhite
■ = Cherry
▨ = Light Blue

Colorwork Chart E

3
2
1

Pattern repeat = 4 stitches

☐ = SuperWhite
▨ = Light Blue

Colorwork Chart SE

3
2
1

Pattern repeat = 2 stitches

☐ = SuperWhite
▨ = Light Blue

Colorwork Chart F

7
6
5
4
3
2
1

Pattern repeat = 4 stitches

☐ = SuperWhite
■ = Cherry
▨ = Light Blue

Colorwork Chart SF

7
6
5
4
3
2
1

Pattern repeat = 2 stitches

☐ = SuperWhite
■ = Cherry
▨ = Light Blue

INSTRUCTIONS

CO 64 sts in Cherry, distribute evenly onto 4 DPNs (16 sts per needle), and join into the round.

For the cuff, work 13 rnds (1.2 in./3 cm) in Cuff Ribbing pattern.

Work the leg in stockinette stitch in Stranded Pattern A in Cherry, Light Blue, and Super-White. Work Rnds 1–55 of the chart once. Break the working yarn in SuperWhite, Cherry, and Light Blue.

Now work a French heel in Cherry in stockinette stitch over the 32 sts of Ndls 4 and 1, following instructions on page 182. Pick up and knit sts from the selvedge of the heel flap in Stranded Pattern SB, alternating 1 st in SuperWhite, 1 st in Light Blue. Work the next-to-last stitch of Ndl 1 and the second stitch of Ndl 4 in SuperWhite. Work the last stitch of Ndl 1 and the first stitch of Ndl 4 in the same stranded pattern as the instep.

Work the foot in stockinette stitch in the round over all sts on all 4 DPNs. Instep (Ndls 2 and 3) and sole of the foot (Ndls 4 and 1) are worked in different stranded patterns. Begin the instep in Stranded Pattern B in Super-White, Light Blue, and Cherry. Work Rnds 1–4 of the chart once. Break the working yarn in Cherry. Then continue in Stranded Pattern C in SuperWhite and Light Blue. Work Rnds 1–3 of the chart 4 times. Now continue in Stranded Pattern D in SuperWhite, Cherry, and Light Blue. Work Rnds 1–11 of the chart once. Break the working yarn in Cherry, and continue in Stranded Pattern E in Super-White and Light Blue. Work Rnds 1–3 of the chart 4 times. Now work Stranded Pattern F in SuperWhite, Cherry, and Light Blue. Work Rnds 1–7 of the chart once. At the same time, begin working the sole in Stranded Pattern SB in SuperWhite, Light Blue, and Cherry. Work Rnds 1–4 of the chart once. Gusset decreases are worked in SuperWhite. Continue to work this stitch in SuperWhite to the end of Stranded Pattern SF. For a neat transition between the sole and the instep, the stranded pattern on the instep begins with the last stitch of Ndl 1 and ends with the first stitch of Ndl 4. Now continue in Stranded Pattern SC in SuperWhite and Light Blue. Work Rnds 1–3 of the chart 4 times. Continue in stranded pattern SD in Super-White, Light Blue, and Cherry. Work Rnds 1–11 of the chart once. Now continue in Stranded Pattern SE in Light Blue and Super-White. Work Rnds 1–3 of the chart 4 times. Now work Stranded Pattern SF in Cherry, SuperWhite, and Light Blue. Work Rnds 1–7 of the chart once.

Break the working yarn in SuperWhite and Light Blue, and finish the sock in Cherry. After 6.9 in./17.5 cm from middle of heel, begin toe decreases.

Work toe with paired banded decreases according to instructions on page 185. Break the working yarn, and pull the end through to the inside of the sock.

Weave in all ends.
Work the second sock the same way.

STITCH COUNTS AND VARIATIONS FOR OTHER SIZES

WOMEN'S 5½–6

CO 64 sts (16 sts per needle).

Foot:

Stranded Patterns B and SB: Work Rnds 1–4 of each chart once.

Stranded Patterns C and SC: Work Rnds 1–3 of each chart 3 times.

Stranded Patterns D and SD: Work Rnds 1–11 of each chart once.

Stranded Patterns E and SE: Work Rnds 1–3 of each chart 3 times.

Stranded Patterns F and SF: Work Rnds 1–7 of each chart once.

Continue as stated in pattern, and after 6.3 in./16 cm from middle of heel, begin toe decreases.

WOMEN'S 9–9½, MEN'S 7–7½

CO 68 sts (17 sts per needle).

Leg: Begin Stranded Pattern A with the fourth stitch; otherwise, the pattern won't align with the pattern on the instep!

Foot:

Stranded Patterns B and SB: Work Rnds 1–4 of each chart once.

Stranded Patterns C and SC: Work Rnds 1–3 of each chart 5 times.

Stranded Patterns D and SD: Work Rnds 1-11 of each chart once.
Stranded Patterns E and SE: Work Rnds 1-3 of each chart 5 times.
Stranded Patterns F and SF: Work Rnds 1-7 of each chart once.
Continue as stated in pattern, and after 7.5 in./19 cm from middle of heel, begin toe decreases.

WOMEN'S 11-12, MEN'S 8½-9

CO 68 sts (17 sts per needle).
Leg: Begin Stranded Pattern A with the fourth stitch; otherwise, the pattern won't align with the pattern on the instep!
Foot:
Stranded Patterns B and SB: Work Rnds 1-4 of each chart once.
Stranded Patterns C and SC: Work Rnds 1-3 of each chart 5 times.
Stranded Patterns D and SD: Work Rnds 1-11 of each chart once.
Stranded Patterns E and SE: Work Rnds 1-3 of each chart 5 times.
Stranded Patterns F and SF: Work Rnds 1-7 of each chart once.
Continue as stated in pattern, and after 8.1 in./20.5 cm from middle of heel, begin toe decreases.

Soxx by

Nature >>>>>>>>>>

SOXX 16

DIFFICULTY LEVEL 3

SIZES

Women's 5½–Men's 11

Pattern instructions as given are for Women's 7–8. Changes to stitch counts and variations needed for other sizes are given on page 100.

MATERIALS

Schachenmayr Regia 4-Ply, super fine (75% wool, 25% polyamide; 230 yd./210 m; 1.75 oz./50 g), 1 skein each in #2140 Bark Heathered, #2080 SuperWhite, and #1945 Light Blue

DPN set of 5 needles in size US 1.5–2.5/2.5–3.0 mm

Cable needle

GAUGE

In colorwork pattern on US 1.5–2.5/2.5–3.0 mm needles, 34 sts and 38 rnds = 4 x 4 in./10 x 10 cm

> Soxx by Nature <

Stranded Patterns A, B, and C

Stitch count has to be a multiple of 4.

Work all rnds in stockinette stitch from the appropriate colorwork chart. Repeat the pattern repeat (4 sts wide) around.

Stranded Pattern A

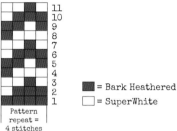

11
10
9
8
7
6
5
4
3
2
1

Pattern repeat = 4 stitches

■ = Bark Heathered
□ = SuperWhite

Stranded Pattern B

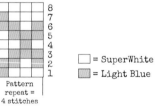

8
7
6
5
4
3
2
1

Pattern repeat = 4 stitches

□ = SuperWhite
▦ = Light Blue

Stranded Pattern C

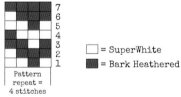

7
6
5
4
3
2
1

Pattern repeat = 4 stitches

□ = SuperWhite
■ = Bark Heathered

Stockinette Stitch

In rows: Knit on RS, purl on WS.

In rnds: Knit all sts in all rnds.

Cuff Ribbing

Stitch count has to be a multiple of 4.

Work all rnds from Cuff Ribbing chart. Repeat the pattern repeat (4 sts wide) around.

Work Rnds 1–3 all the time, unless stated otherwise in the instructions.

Rnds 1 and 2: Alternate "k3, p1."

Rnd 3: Hold 2 sts on cable needle in front of work, knit 1; then knit 2 from cable needle, purl 1.

Cuff Ribbing

3
2
1

■ = knit 1

– = purl 1

= Hold 2 sts on cable needle in front of work, knit 1; then knit 2 from cable needle.

INSTRUCTIONS

CO 64 sts in Bark Heathered, distribute evenly onto 4 DPNs (16 sts per needle), and join into the round.

For the cuff, work 23 rnds (1.8 in./4.5 cm) in Cuff Ribbing pattern. Work Rnds 1–3 of the chart 7 times; then repeat only Rnds 1 and 2 once.

Now work the leg in stockinette stitch in Stranded Pattern A in Bark Heathered and SuperWhite. Work Rnds 1–11 of the chart once. Break the working yarn in Bark Heath-ered. Now work Stranded Pattern B in Super-White and Light Blue. Work Rnds 1–8 of the chart 3 times; then work 1 more rnd in SuperWhite. Break the working yarn in Light Blue and SuperWhite.

Now work a boomerang heel in stockinette stitch in Bark Heathered over the 32 sts of Ndls 4 and 1, following instructions on page 179. Break the working yarn in Bark Heath-ered.

WOMEN'S 5½–6

CO 64 sts (16 sts per needle).

Foot, Stranded Pattern B: Work Rnds 1–8 of the chart 3 times and Rnds 1–7 once. Continue as stated in pattern, and after 7.3 in./18.5 cm from middle of heel, start decreases for the rounded toe.

WOMEN'S 9–9½, MEN'S 7–7½

CO 68 sts (17 sts per needle).

Foot, Stranded Pattern B: Work Rnds 1–8 of the chart 5 times and Rnds 1–7 once. Continue as stated in pattern, and after 8.5 in./21.5 cm from middle of heel, start decreases for the rounded toe.

WOMEN'S 11–12, MEN'S 8½–9

CO 68 sts (17 sts per needle).

Foot, Stranded Pattern B: Work Rnds 1–8 of the chart 5 times and Rnds 1–7 once. Continue as stated in pattern, and after 9.1 in./23 cm from middle of heel, start decreases for the rounded toe.

MEN'S 10–11

CO 72 sts (18 sts per needle).

Foot, Stranded Pattern B: Work Rnds 1–8 of the chart 5 times and Rnds 1–7 once. Continue as stated in pattern, and after 9.6 in./24.5 cm from middle of heel, start decreases for the rounded toe.

Work the foot in stockinette stitch in the round over all sts on all 4 DPNs. Begin with 2 rnds in SuperWhite; then work Stranded Pattern B in SuperWhite and Light Blue. Work Rnds 1–8 of the chart 4 times; then work only Rnds 1–7 once more. Break the working yarn in Light Blue, and continue in Stranded Pattern C in SuperWhite and Bark Heathered. Work Rnds 1–7 once. Break the working yarn in SuperWhite, and finish the sock in Bark Heathered. After 8 in./20 cm from middle of heel, start decreases for the rounded toe.

Work a rounded toe according to instructions on page 185. Graft the remaining opening in Kitchener stitch (see page 186).

Weave in all ends.

Work the second sock the same way.

SOXX 17

DIFFICULTY LEVEL 2

SIZES

Women's 9–Men's 13

Pattern instructions as given are for Women's 11–12 and Men's 8½–9. Changes to stitch counts and variations needed for other sizes are given on page 107.

MATERIALS

Lana Grossa Meilenweit 50, super fine (80% wool, 20% nylon; 230 yd./210 m; 1.75 oz./50 g), 1 skein each in #1359 Light Brown Heathered, #1302 Pastel Blue Heathered, and #1301 Beige Heathered

DPN set of 5 needles in size US 1.5–2.5/2.5–3.0 mm

GAUGE

In stockinette stitch on US 1.5–2.5/2.5–3.0 mm needles, 32 sts and 40 rnds = 4 x 4 in./10 x 10 cm

Stockinette Stitch

In rows: Knit on RS, purl on WS.
In rnds: Knit all sts in all rnds.

Cuff Ribbing

Alternate "k1, p1."

Stranded Patterns A, B, C, and D

Stitch count has to be a multiple of 4.
Work all rnds in stockinette stitch from the
appropriate colorwork chart. Repeat the
pattern repeat (4 sts wide) around.

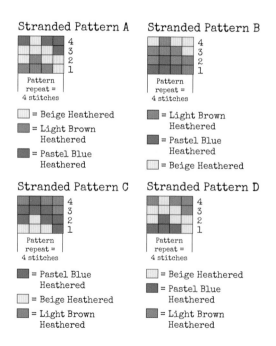

Stranded Pattern A

Pattern
repeat =
4 stitches

☐ = Beige Heathered

▨ = Light Brown
Heathered

■ = Pastel Blue
Heathered

Stranded Pattern B

Pattern
repeat =
4 stitches

▨ = Light Brown
Heathered

■ = Pastel Blue
Heathered

☐ = Beige Heathered

Stranded Pattern C

Pattern
repeat =
4 stitches

■ = Pastel Blue
Heathered

☐ = Beige Heathered

▨ = Light Brown
Heathered

Stranded Pattern D

Pattern
repeat =
4 stitches

☐ = Beige Heathered

■ = Pastel Blue
Heathered

▨ = Light Brown
Heathered

INSTRUCTIONS

CO 64 sts in Light Brown Heathered, distribute
evenly onto 4 DPNs (16 sts per needle), and
join into the round.

For the cuff, work 13 rnds (1.2 in./3 cm) in Cuff
Ribbing pattern.

Work the leg in stockinette stitch, beginning
with 7 rnds in Light Brown Heathered. Now
continue in Stranded Pattern A in Beige
Heathered, Light Brown Heathered, and
Pastel Blue Heathered. Work Rnds 1–4 of the
chart once. Break the working yarn in Light
Brown Heathered and Beige Heathered.
Then work 15 rnds in Pastel Blue Heathered.
Now work Stranded Pattern B in Light Brown
Heathered, Pastel Blue Heathered, and Beige
Heathered. Work Rnds 1–4 of the chart once.
Break the working yarn in Pastel Blue Heath-
ered and Light Brown Heathered. Then work
15 rnds in Beige Heathered. Now continue in
Stranded Pattern C in Pastel Blue Heathered,
Beige Heathered, and Light Brown Heath-
ered. Work Rnds 1–4 of the chart once. Break
the working yarn in Beige Heathered and
Pastel Blue Heathered. Now work 15 rnds in
Light Brown Heathered. Then continue in
Stranded Pattern A in Beige Heathered, Light
Brown Heathered, and Pastel Blue Heathered. Work Rnds 1–4 of the chart once. Break
the working yarn in Light Brown Heathered
and Beige Heathered, and finish the leg with
3 rnds in Pastel Blue Heathered.

Now work a French heel in Pastel Blue Heathered in stockinette stitch over the 32 sts of
Ndls 4 and 1 according to instructions on
page 182.

Continue the foot in Pastel Blue Heathered in stockinette stitch in the round over all sts on all 4 DPNs. After 6.5 in./16.5 cm from middle of heel, begin Stranded Pattern D in Beige Heathered, Pastel Blue Heathered, and Light Brown Heathered. Work Rnds 1–4 of the chart once. Break the working yarn in Pastel Blue Heathered and Beige Heathered, and

finish the sock in Light Brown Heathered. After 8.1 in./20.5 cm from middle of heel, begin toe decreases.

Work toe with paired banded decreases according to instructions on page 185. Break the working yarn, and pull the end through to the inside of the sock.

Weave in all ends.

Work the second sock the same way.

STITCH COUNTS AND VARIATIONS FOR OTHER SIZES

WOMEN'S 9–9½, MEN'S 7–7½
CO 64 sts (16 sts per needle).
Foot: After 5.9 in./15 cm from middle of heel, begin Stranded Pattern D. Work Rnds 1-4 of the chart once. Continue as stated in pattern, and after 7.5 in./19 cm from middle of heel, begin toe decreases.

MEN'S 10–11
CO 68 sts (17 sts per needle).
Foot: After 7.1 in./18 cm from middle of heel, begin Stranded Pattern D. Work Rnds 1-4 of the chart once. Continue as stated in pattern, and after 8.7 in./22 cm from middle of heel, begin toe decreases.

MEN'S 12–13
CO 72 sts (18 sts per needle).
Foot: After 7.7 in./19.5 cm from middle of heel, begin Stranded Pattern D. Work Rnds 1-4 of the chart once. Continue as stated in pattern, and after 9.3 in./23.5 cm from middle of heel, begin toe decreases.

SOXX 18

DIFFICULTY LEVEL 3

SIZES

Child's 1–10

Pattern instructions as given are for Child's 4–5, foot
length approximately 5.5 in./14 cm. Changes to stitch
counts and variations needed for other sizes are given
on page 112.

MATERIALS

Lang Yarns Jawoll, super fine (75% wool, 25% nylon;
230 yd./210 m; 1.75 oz./50 g), 1 skein each in #372
Aqua, #94 Off-White, and #339 Camel

DPN set of 5 needles in size US 1.5–2.5/2.5–3.0 mm

GAUGE

In colorwork pattern on US 1.5–2.5/2.5–3.0 mm needles,
36 sts and 38 rnds = 4 x 4 in./10 x 10 cm

Stockinette Stitch

In rows: Knit on RS, purl on WS.
In rnds: Knit all sts in all rnds.

Cuff Ribbing

Alternate "k2, p2."

Stranded Patterns A, B, C, and D

Stitch count has to be a multiple of 4.
Work all rnds in stockinette stitch from the appropriate colorwork chart. Repeat the pattern repeat (4 sts wide) around.

Stranded Pattern A

6
5
4
3
2
1

■ = Camel
☐ = Off-White

Pattern
repeat =
4 stitches

SOCK 1 ONLY

Stranded Pattern B

4
3
2
1

Pattern
repeat =
4 stitches

☐ = Off-White
▨ = Aqua

Stranded Pattern C

4
3
2
1

Pattern
repeat =
4 stitches

▨ = Camel
☐ = Off-White

SOCK 2 ONLY

Stranded Pattern D

4
3
2
1

Pattern
repeat =
4 stitches

☐ = Off-White
▨ = Aqua

Stranded Pattern E

4
3
2
1

Pattern
repeat =
4 stitches

☐ = Off-White
▨ = Camel

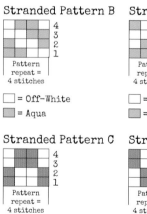

INSTRUCTIONS

CO 52 sts in Camel, distribute evenly onto 4 DPNs (13 sts per needle), and join into the round.

For the cuff, work 10 rnds in Camel (0.6 in./1.5 cm) in Cuff Ribbing pattern.

Begin the leg in Stranded Pattern A in Camel and Off-White. Work Rnds 1–6 of the chart once. Break the working yarn in Camel.

SOCK 1: Continue in Stranded Pattern B in Off-White and Aqua. Work Rnds 1–4 of the chart 5 times. Break the working yarn in both colors.

SOCK 2: Continue in Stranded Pattern D in Off-White and Aqua. Work Rnds 1–4 of the chart 5 times. Break the working yarn in both colors.

Now work a boomerang heel in Camel in stockinette stitch over the 26 sts of Ndls 4 and 1, following instructions on page 179. Then break the working yarn.

Work the foot in stockinette stitch in the round over all sts on all 4 DPNs.

SOCK 1: Continue in Stranded Pattern B in Off-White and Aqua. Work Rnds 1–4 of the chart 5 times. Break the working yarn in Aqua. Then continue in Stranded Pattern C in Camel and Off-White. Work Rnds 1–4 of the chart once.

CHILD'S 1, foot length approximately 5 in./12.5 cm
CO 48 sts (12 sts per needle).
Leg, Stranded Pattern B (Sock 1) or D (Sock 2): Work Rnds 1–4, 4 times.
Foot, Stranded Pattern B (Sock 1) or D (Sock 2): Work Rnds 1–4, 4 times.
Foot, Stranded Pattern C (Sock 1) or E (Sock 2): Work Rnds 1 and 2 once.
Continue as stated in pattern, and after 4 in./10 cm from middle of
heel, start decreases for the rounded toe.

CHILD'S 2–3, foot length approximately 5.5 in./14 cm
CO 48 sts (12 sts per needle).
Foot, Stranded Pattern B (Sock 1) or D (Sock 2): Work Rnds 1–4, 5 times.
Foot, Stranded Pattern C (Sock 1) or E (Sock 2): Work Rnds 1–4 once.
Continue as stated in pattern, and after 4.5 in./11.5 cm from middle
of heel, start decreases for the rounded toe.

CHILD'S 6–7, foot length approximately 6.5 in./16.5 cm
CO 52 sts (13 sts per needle).
Foot, Stranded Pattern B (Sock 1) or D (Sock 2): Work Rnds 1–4, 7 times.
Foot, Stranded Pattern C (Sock 1) or E (Sock 2): Work Rnds 1–4 once.
Continue as stated in pattern, and after 5.5 in./14 cm from middle of
heel, start decreases for the rounded toe.

CHILD'S 8–10, foot length approximately 7.1 in./18 cm
CO 56 sts (14 sts per needle).
Leg, Stranded Pattern B (Sock 1) or D (Sock 2): Work Rnds 1–4, 8 times.
Foot, Stranded Pattern B (Sock 1) or D (Sock 2): Work Rnds 1–4, 8 times.
Foot, Stranded Pattern C (Sock 1) or E (Sock 2): Work Rnds 1–4 once.
Continue as stated in pattern, and after 6 in./15 cm from middle of
heel, start decreases for the rounded toe.

SOCK 2: Continue in Stranded Pattern D in Off-White and Aqua. Work Rnds 1–4 of the chart 5 times. Break the working yarn in Aqua. Then continue in Stranded Pattern E in Off-White and Camel. Work Rnds 1–4 of the chart once.

Break the working yarn in Off-White, and finish the sock in Camel. After 5 in./12.5 cm from middle of heel, start decreases for the rounded toe.

Work a rounded toe according to instructions on page 185. Graft the remaining opening in Kitchener stitch (see page 186). Weave in all ends.

Please note: On the book cover, the same socks are shown knit in Lang Yarns Jawoll yarn in #01 White, #159 Tangerine, and #220 Pastel Blue.

SOXX 19

DIFFICULTY LEVEL 1

SIZES

Women's 5½–Men's 11

Pattern instructions as given are for Women's 7–8. Changes to stitch counts and variations needed for other sizes are given on page 117.

MATERIALS FOR TWO PAIRS OF SOCKS

Schachenmayr Regia Premium Merino Yak, super fine (58% wool, 28% polyamide, 14% yak; 437 yd./400 m, 3.5 oz./100 g per skein), 1 skein each #7507 Raspberry Heathered and #7510 Beige Heathered

DPN set of 5 needles in size US 1.5–2.5/2.5–3.0 mm

GAUGE

In stockinette stitch on US 1.5–2.5/2.5–3.0 mm needles, 32 sts and 42 rnds = 4 x 4 in./10 x 10 cm

Stockinette Stitch

In rows: Knit on RS, purl on WS.
In rnds: Knit all sts in all rnds.

Cuff Ribbing

Alternate "k1, p1."

Knit-Purl Pattern

Stitch count has to be a multiple of 4.
Work in rnds from the chart. Repeat the pattern
    repeat (4 sts wide) around.
Rnd 1: * Alternate "k3, p1," rep from * around.

Knit-Purl Pattern

| – | ■ | ■ | ■ | 1 |

■ = knit 1
– = purl 1

INSTRUCTIONS

CO 60 sts in Raspberry Heathered, distribute
    evenly onto 4 DPNs (15 sts per needle), and
    join into the round.
For the cuff, work 10 rnds (0.8 in./2 cm) in Cuff
    Ribbing pattern.
For the leg, work 5.1 in./13 cm in knit-purl pat-
    tern.
Now work a boomerang heel in stockinette
    stitch over the 30 sts of Ndls 4 and 1, follow-
    ing instructions on page 179, working the
    first half of the heel and Rnd 1 over all sts in
    Raspberry Heathered; then break the work-
    ing yarn. Now work Rnd 2 over all sts, work-
    ing the second half of the heel in Beige
    Heathered. In the two rnds worked over all

sts, continue the knit-purl pattern over the
    instep stitches (Ndls 2 and 3).
Continue the foot in Beige Heathered in the
    round over all sts on all 4 DPNs. Work the sts
    of Ndls 1 and 4 (sole) in stockinette stitch.
    Continue the knit-purl pattern over the
    instep stitches (Ndls 2 and 3). Keep in this
    pattern to the end of the sock. After 5.9
    in./15 cm from middle of heel, work stripe
    sequence * 2 rnds in Raspberry Heathered, 3
    rnds in Beige Heathered; rep from * to end of
    sock, starting banded toe decreases after 6.9
    in./17.5 cm from middle of heel.
Work toe with paired banded decreases accord-
    ing to instructions on page 185, making sure
    to continue the knit-purl pattern on the
    instep to the end. Break the working yarn in
    all colors, and pull the ends through to the
    inside of the sock.
Weave in all ends.
Work the second sock the same way.

Tip: To make a second pair of socks from the
    remainder of your yarn, invert the colors.

STITCH COUNTS AND VARIATIONS FOR OTHER SIZES

WOMEN'S 5½–6
CO 60 sts (15 sts per needle).
Foot: After 5.3 in./13.5 cm from middle of heel, begin stripe sequence as instructed, and after 6.3 in./16 cm from middle of heel, begin toe decreases.

WOMEN'S 9–9½, MEN'S 7–7½
CO 64 sts (16 sts per needle).
Foot: After 6.5 in./16.5 cm from middle of heel, begin stripe sequence as instructed, and after 7.5 in./19 cm from middle of heel, begin toe decreases.

WOMEN'S 11–12, MEN'S 8½–9
CO 64 sts (16 sts per needle).
Foot: After 7.1 in./18 cm from middle of heel, begin stripe sequence as instructed, and after 8.1 in./20.5 cm from middle of heel, begin toe decreases.

MEN'S 10–11
CO 68 sts (17 sts per needle).
Foot: After 7.7 in./19.5 cm from middle of heel, begin stripe sequence as instructed, and after 8.7 in./22 cm from middle of heel, begin toe decreases.

SoXX 20

DIFFICULTY LEVEL 2

SIZES

Women's 9–Men's 13

Pattern instructions as given are for Women's 11–12 and Men's 8½–9. Changes to stitch counts and variations needed for other sizes are given on page 120.

MATERIALS

Schachenmayr Regia 4-Ply, super fine (75% wool, 25% polyamide; 230 yd./210 m; 1.75 oz./50 g), 1 skein each in #522 Anthracite Heathered, #2070 Wood Streaked, and #2002 Cherry, and a small amount of #2080 Super-White (*Note: For Men's 10–11 and larger, 2 skeins of Wood Streaked are needed.*)

DPN set of 5 needles in size US 1.5–2.5/2.5–3.0 mm

GAUGE

In colorwork pattern on US 1.5–2.5/2.5–3.0 mm needles, 34 sts and 38 rnds = 4 x 4 in./10 x 10 cm

WOMEN'S 9–9½, MEN'S 7–7½
CO 68 sts (17 sts per needle).
Foot: After 5.3 in./13.5 cm, begin stranded pattern. Work Rnds 7–17 and Rnds 1–3 of the chart once each. After 7.5 in./19 cm from middle of heel, begin toe decreases.

Note: For Men's 10–11 and larger, 2 skeins of Wood Streaked are needed.

MEN'S 10–11
CO 72 sts (18 sts per needle).
Foot: After 6.5 in./16.5 cm, begin stranded pattern. Work Rnds 7–17 and Rnds 1–3 of the chart once each. After 8.7 in./22 cm from middle of heel, begin toe decreases.

MEN'S 12–13
CO 76 sts (19 sts per needle).
Foot: After 7.1 in./18 cm, begin stranded pattern. Work Rnds 7–17 and Rnds 1–3 of the chart once each. After 9.3 in./23.5 cm from middle of heel, begin toe decreases.

Stockinette Stitch

In rows: Knit on RS, purl on WS.
In rnds: Knit all sts in all rnds.

Cuff Ribbing

Alternate "k1, p1."

Stranded Pattern

Stitch count has to be a multiple of 4.
Work all rnds in stockinette stitch from the colorwork chart. Repeat the pattern repeat (4 sts wide) around.

Colorwork Chart

Pattern repeat = 4 stitches

■ = Anthracite Heathered
▨ = Wood Streaked
■ = Cherry
☐ = SuperWhite

INSTRUCTIONS

CO 68 sts in Anthracite Heathered, distribute evenly onto 4 DPNs (17 sts per needle), and join into the round.

For the cuff, work 15 rnds (1.4 in./3.5 cm) in Cuff Ribbing pattern.

Work the leg in stranded pattern in Anthracite Heathered, Wood Streaked, Cherry, and SuperWhite. Work Rnds 1–17 of the chart twice; then repeat only Rnds 1–6 once. Break the working yarn in Anthracite Heathered, Cherry, and SuperWhite, and finish the leg with 5 rnds in Wood Streaked.

Now work a French heel in Wood Streaked in stockinette stitch over the 34 sts of Ndls 4 and 1 according to instructions on page 182.

Work the foot in stockinette stitch in the round over all sts on all 4 DPNs in Wood Streaked.

After 5.9 in./15 cm from middle of heel, continue in stranded pattern in Wood Streaked, Cherry, SuperWhite, and Anthracite Heathered. Work Rnds 7–17 and Rnds 1–3 of the chart once each. Break the working yarn in Wood Streaked, Cherry, and SuperWhite, and finish the sock in Anthracite Heathered. After 8.1 in./20.5 cm from middle of heel, begin toe decreases.

Work toe with paired banded decreases according to instructions on page 185. Break the working yarn, and pull the end through to the inside of the sock.

Weave in all ends.

Work the second sock the same way.

Be-My-Valentine

Soxx >>>>>>>>>>>>>>>>>>>>

SOXX 21

DIFFICULTY LEVEL 3

SIZES

Women's 5½–Men's 11

Pattern instructions as given are for Women's 7–8.
Changes to stitch counts and variations needed for other
sizes are given on page 129.

MATERIALS

Lang Yarns Jawoll, super fine (75% wool, 25% nylon;
230 yd./210 m; 1.75 oz./50 g), 1 skein each in #390 Dark
Eggplant, #150 Gold, #119 Pink, and #226 Beige

DPN set of 5 needles in size US 1.5–2.5/2.5–3.0 mm

GAUGE

In colorwork pattern on US 1.5–2.5/2.5–3.0 mm needles,
34 sts and 42 rnds = 4 x 4 in./10 x 10 cm

Stockinette Stitch

In rows: Knit on RS, purl on WS.
In rnds: Knit all sts in all rnds.

Knitting through the Back Loop (k-tbl)

Insert the needle from right to left into the back
leg of the stitch; knit the stitch this way so it
ends up twisted.

Cuff Ribbing

Alternate "k1-tbl, p1."

Stranded Patterns A and B

Stitch count has to be a multiple of 4.
Work all rnds in stockinette stitch from the
appropriate colorwork chart. Repeat the
pattern repeat (4 sts wide) around.

Stranded Pattern A

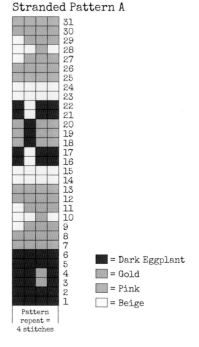

■ = Dark Eggplant
▨ = Gold
▧ = Pink
☐ = Beige

Pattern
repeat =
4 stitches

Stranded Pattern B

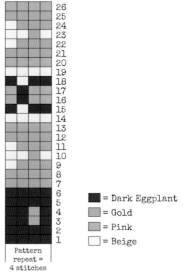

■ = Dark Eggplant
▨ = Gold
▧ = Pink
☐ = Beige

Pattern
repeat =
4 stitches

INSTRUCTIONS

CO 64 sts in Pink, distribute evenly onto 4 DPNs (16 sts per needle), and join into the round.

For the cuff, work 6 rnds in Pink, 3 rnds in Beige, and 3 rnds in Dark Eggplant (1 in./2.5 cm) in Cuff Ribbing pattern.

Work the leg in stockinette stitch in Stranded Pattern A in Dark Eggplant, Gold, Pink, and Beige. Work Rnds 3–31 of the chart once; then work Rnds 1–31 once. Break the working yarn in all colors.

Now work a boomerang heel in stockinette stitch in Dark Eggplant over the 32 sts of Ndls 4 and 1 according to instructions on page 179.

Work the foot in stockinette stitch in the round over all sts on all 4 DPNs. Work Stranded Pattern B in Dark Eggplant, Gold, Pink, and Beige. Work Rnds 3–26 of the chart once; then work Rnds 1–26 once. Break the working yarn in Gold, Pink, and Beige, and finish

the sock in Dark Eggplant. After 8 in./20 cm from middle of heel, start decreases for the rounded toe.

Work a rounded toe according to instructions on page 185. Graft the remaining opening in Kitchener stitch (see page 186).

Weave in all ends.

Work the second sock the same way.

STITCH COUNTS AND VARIATIONS FOR OTHER SIZES

WOMEN'S 5½–6
CO 64 sts (16 sts per needle).
Foot, Stranded Pattern B: Work Rnds 3–26 of the chart once and then Rnds 1–20 once. Continue as stated in pattern, and after 7.3 in./18.5 cm from middle of heel, start decreases for the rounded toe.

WOMEN'S 9–9½, MEN'S 7–7½
CO 68 sts (17 sts per needle).
Foot, Stranded Pattern B: Work Rnds 3–26 of the chart once and then Rnds 1–26 once; then repeat only Rnds 1–7 once more. Continue as stated in pattern, and after 8.5 in./21.5 cm from middle of heel, start decreases for the rounded toe.

WOMEN'S 11–12, MEN'S 8½–9
CO 68 sts (17 sts per needle).
Foot, Stranded Pattern B: Work Rnds 3–26 of the chart once and Rnds 1–26 once; then repeat only Rnds 1–13 once more. Continue as stated in pattern, and after 9.1 in./23 cm from middle of heel, start decreases for the rounded toe.

MEN'S 10–11
CO 72 sts (18 sts per needle).
Foot, Stranded Pattern B: Work Rnds 3–26 of the chart once and Rnds 1–26 once; then repeat only Rnds 1–20 once more. Continue as stated in pattern, and after 9.6 in./24.5 cm from middle of heel, start decreases for the rounded toe.

SOXX 22

DIFFICULTY LEVEL 2

SIZES

Women's 5½–Men's 11

Pattern instructions as given are for Women's 7–8. Changes to stitch counts and variations needed for other sizes are given on page 133.

MATERIALS

Lang Yarns Jawoll, super fine (75% wool, 25% nylon; 230 yd./210 m; 1.75 oz./50 g), 2 skeins #23 Light Grey Heathered, 1 skein #184 Azalea, and a small amount of #228 Salmon

DPN set of 5 needles in size US 1.5–2.5/2.5–3.0 mm

GAUGE

In stockinette stitch on US 1.5–2.5/2.5–3.0 mm needles, 32 sts and 44 rnds = 4 x 4 in./10 x 10 cm

Stockinette Stitch

In rows: Knit on RS, purl on WS.
In rnds: Knit all sts in all rnds.

Cuff Ribbing

Alternate "k1, p1."

Stranded Pattern

Stitch count has to be a multiple of 4.
Work all rnds in stockinette stitch from the colorwork chart. Repeat the pattern repeat (4 sts wide) around.

Colorwork Chart

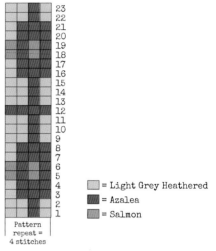

□ = Light Grey Heathered
▨ = Azalea
▨ = Salmon

Pattern
repeat =
4 stitches

INSTRUCTIONS

CO 60 sts in Azalea, distribute evenly onto 4 DPNs (15 sts per needle), and join into the round.

For the cuff, work 2 rnds in Azalea and 10 rnds in Light Grey Heathered in Cuff Ribbing pattern (1 in./2.5 cm). Break the working yarn in Azalea.

Work the leg in stockinette stitch, beginning with 15 rnds in Light Grey Heathered; then continue in stranded pattern in Light Grey Heathered, Azalea, and Salmon. Work Rnds 1–23 of the chart once. Break the working yarn in Azalea and Salmon. Then work 15 rnds in Light Grey Heathered.

Now work a French heel in Light Grey Heathered over the 30 sts of Ndls 4 and 1, following instructions on page 182.

Work the foot in stockinette stitch in the round over all sts on all 4 DPNs. Begin with 20 rnds in Light Grey Heathered; then continue in stranded pattern in Light Grey Heathered, Azalea, and Salmon. Work Rnds 1–23 of the chart once. Break the working yarn in Azalea and Salmon, and finish the sock in Light Grey Heathered. After 6.9 in./17.5 cm from middle of heel, begin toe decreases.

Work toe with paired banded decreases according to instructions on page 185. Break the working yarn, and pull the end through to the inside of the sock.

Weave in all ends.

Work the second sock the same way.

STITCH COUNTS AND VARIATIONS FOR OTHER SIZES

WOMEN'S 5½–6
CO 60 sts (15 sts per needle).
Foot: Begin with 16 rnds in Light Grey Heathered. Continue as stated in pattern, and after 6.3 in./16 cm from middle of heel, begin toe decreases.

WOMEN'S 9–9½, MEN'S 7–7½
CO 64 sts (16 sts per needle).
Foot: Begin with 24 rnds in Light Grey Heathered. Continue as stated in pattern, and after 7.5 in./19 cm from middle of heel, begin toe decreases.

WOMEN'S 11–12, MEN'S 8½–9
CO 64 sts (16 sts per needle).
Foot: Begin with 28 rnds in Light Grey Heathered. Continue as stated in pattern, and after 8.1 in./20.5 cm from middle of heel, begin toe decreases.

MEN'S 10–11
CO 68 sts (17 sts per needle).
Foot: Begin with 32 rnds in Light Grey Heathered. Continue as stated in pattern, and after 8.7 in./22 cm from middle of heel, begin toe decreases.

SOXX 23

DIFFICULTY LEVEL 2

SIZES

Child's 1–7

Pattern instructions as given are for Child's 4–5, foot length approximately 5.5 in./14 cm. Changes to stitch counts and variations needed for other sizes are given on page 137.

MATERIALS

Schachenmayr Baby Smiles My First Regia, super fine (75% wool, 25% polyamide; 115 yd./105 m, 0.9 oz./25 g per skein); 1 skein each in #1002 Nature, #1053 Sky Blue, and #1047 Orchid

DPN set of 5 needles in size US 1.5–2.5/2.5–3.0 mm

GAUGE

In colorwork pattern on US 1.5–2.5/2.5–3.0 mm needles, 32 sts and 44 rnds = 4 x 4 in./10 x 10 cm

INSTRUCTIONS

CO 52 sts in Orchid, distribute evenly onto 4 DPNs (13 sts per needle), and join into the round.

For the cuff, work 7 rnds (0.6 in./1.5 cm) in Cuff Ribbing pattern.

Work the leg in stockinette stitch, beginning with 1 rnd in Nature. Then work stranded pattern in Nature, Sky Blue, and Orchid. Work Rnds 1–14 of the chart twice. Now work * 1 rnd in Nature, 1 rnd in Orchid; rep from * once. Break the working yarn in all colors.

Now work a boomerang heel in stockinette stitch in Sky Blue over the 26 sts of Ndls 4 and 1, following instructions on page 179.

Work the foot in stockinette stitch in the round over all sts on all 4 DPNs. Alternate "1 rnd in Orchid, 1 rnd in Nature," until a length of 4.7 in./12 cm from middle of heel has been reached. Work 1 more rnd in Orchid; then break the working yarn in both colors. Finish the sock in Sky Blue. After 5 in./12.5 cm from middle of heel, start toe decreases for the rounded toe.

Work a rounded toe according to instructions on page 185. Graft the remaining opening in Kitchener stitch (see page 186).

Weave in all ends.

Work the second sock the same way.

Stockinette Stitch

In rows: Knit on RS, purl on WS.
In rnds: Knit all sts in all rnds.

Knitting through the Back Loop (k-tbl)

Insert the needle from right to left into the back leg of the stitch; knit the stitch this way so it ends up twisted.

Cuff Ribbing

Alternate "k1-tbl, p1."

Stranded Pattern

Stitch count has to be a multiple of 4.
Work all rnds in stockinette stitch from the colorwork chart. Repeat the pattern repeat (4 sts wide) around.

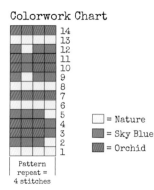

Colorwork Chart

☐ = Nature
▓ = Sky Blue
▨ = Orchid

Pattern repeat = 4 stitches

STITCH COUNTS AND VARIATIONS FOR OTHER SIZES

CHILD'S 1, foot length approximately 5 in./12.5 cm
CO 48 sts (12 sts per needle).
Leg, stranded pattern: Work Rnds 1–14 of the chart once and Rnds 1–7 once.
Foot: After 3.75 in./9.5 cm from middle of heel, work 1 more rnd in Orchid; then break working yarn in Nature and Orchid. Finish the sock in Sky Blue, and after 4 in./10 cm from middle of heel, start decreases for the rounded toe.

CHILD'S 2–3, foot length approximately 5.5 in./14 cm
CO 48 sts (12 sts per needle).
Foot: After 4.3 in./11 cm from middle of heel, work 1 more rnd in Orchid; then break working yarn in Nature and Orchid. Finish the sock in Sky Blue, and after 4.5 in./11.5 cm from middle of heel, start decreases for the rounded toe.

CHILD'S 6–7, foot length approximately 6.5 in./16.5 cm
CO 52 sts (13 sts per needle).
Foot: After 5.3 in./13.5 cm from middle of heel, work 1 more rnd in Orchid; then break working yarn in Nature and Orchid. Finish the sock in Sky Blue, and after 5.5 in./14 cm from middle of heel, start decreases for the rounded toe.

SOXX 24

DIFFICULTY LEVEL 2

SIZES

Women's 5½–Men's 11

Pattern instructions as given are for Women's 7–8. Changes to stitch counts and variations needed for other sizes are given on page 141.

MATERIALS

Lana Grossa Meilenweit 50, super fine (80% wool, 20% nylon; 230 yd./210 m; 1.75 oz./50 g), 1 skein each in #1313 Pink and #1301 Beige Heathered

DPN set of 5 needles in size US 1.5–2.5/2.5–3.0 mm

GAUGE

In stockinette stitch on US 1.5–2.5/2.5–3.0 mm needles, 32 sts and 46 rnds = 4 x 4 in./10 x 10 cm

Stockinette Stitch

In rows: Knit on RS, purl on WS.
In rnds: Knit all sts in all rnds.

Cuff Ribbing

Alternate "k2, p2."

Stranded Patterns A and B

Stitch count has to be a multiple of 4.
Work all rnds in stockinette stitch from the
appropriate colorwork chart. Repeat the
pattern repeat (4 sts wide) around.

Stranded Pattern A

Pattern repeat = 4 stitches

■ = Pink
□ = Beige Heathered

Stranded Pattern B

Pattern repeat = 4 stitches

□ = Beige Heathered
■ = Pink

INSTRUCTIONS

CO 60 sts in Pink, distribute evenly onto 4 DPNs
(15 sts per needle), and join into the round.

For the cuff, work 15 rnds (1.4 in./3.5 cm) in Cuff
Ribbing pattern.

Begin the leg with 15 rnds in Pink; then continue in Stranded Pattern A in Pink and Beige
Heathered. Work Rnds 1–4 of the chart once.
Break the working yarn in Pink, and work 22
rnds in Beige Heathered. Now work Stranded
Pattern B in Beige Heathered and Pink. Work
Rnds 1–4 of the chart once. Then break the
working yarn in Beige Heathered, and work
10 rnds in Pink.

Now work a boomerang heel in Pink in stockinette stitch over the 30 sts of Ndls 4 and 1,
following instructions on page 179.

Work the foot in stockinette stitch in the round
over all sts on all 4 DPNs. Start with 10 rnds
in Pink, followed by Stranded Pattern A in

Pink and Beige Heathered. Work Rnds 1–4 of
the chart once.

Break the working yarn in Pink. Work 22 rnds in
Beige Heathered; then work Stranded Pattern B in Beige Heathered and Pink. Work
Rnds 1–4 of the chart once. Break the working yarn in Beige Heathered, and finish the
sock in Pink. After 6.9 in./17.5 cm from middle of heel, begin toe decreases.

Work toe with paired banded decreases according to instructions on page 185. Break the
working yarn, and pull the end through to
the inside of the sock.

Weave in all ends.

Work the second sock the same way.

STITCH COUNTS AND VARIATIONS FOR OTHER SIZES

WOMEN'S 5½–6
CO 60 sts (15 sts per needle).
Foot: After 6.3 in./16 cm from middle of heel, begin toe decreases.

WOMEN'S 9–9½, MEN'S 7–7½
CO 64 sts (16 sts per needle).
Foot: After having completed Stranded Pattern A, break the working yarn in Pink, and work 28 rnds in Beige Heathered. Continue as stated in pattern, and after 7.5 in./19 cm from middle of heel, begin toe decreases.

WOMEN'S 11–12, MEN'S 8½–9
CO 64 sts (16 sts per needle).
Foot: After having completed Stranded Pattern A, break the working yarn in Pink, and work 34 rnds in Beige Heathered. Continue as stated in pattern, and after 8.1 in./20.5 cm from middle of heel, begin toe decreases.

MEN'S 10–11
CO 68 sts (17 sts per needle).
Foot: After having completed Stranded Pattern A, break the working yarn in Pink, and work 40 rnds in Beige Heathered. Continue as stated in pattern, and after 8.7 in./22 cm from middle of heel, begin toe decreases.

SOXX 25

DIFFICULTY LEVEL 2

SIZES

Women's 5½–Men's 11

Pattern instructions as given are for Women's 7–8. Changes to stitch counts and variations needed for other sizes are given on page 147.

MATERIALS

Lana Grossa Meilenweit 50, super fine (80% wool, 20% nylon; 230 yd./210 m; 1.75 oz./50 g), 1 skein #1313 Pink and #1102 Beige-Grey Heathered (*Note: For Women's 11–12, Men's 8½–9, and larger, 2 skeins of Pink are needed.*)

DPN set of 5 needles in size US 1.5–2.5/2.5–3.0 mm

GAUGE

In colorwork pattern on US 1.5–2.5/2.5–3.0 mm needles, 34 sts and 38 rnds = 4 x 4 in./10 x 10 cm

Stockinette Stitch

In rows: Knit on RS, purl on WS.
In rnds: Knit all sts in all rnds.

Knitting through the Back Loop (k-tbl)

Insert the needle from right to left into the back
    leg of the stitch; knit the stitch this way so it
    ends up twisted.

Cuff Ribbing

Alternate "k1-tbl, p1."

Stranded Patterns A, B, and C

Stitch count has to be a multiple of 4.
Work all rnds in stockinette stitch from the
    appropriate colorwork chart. Repeat the
    pattern repeat (4 sts wide) around.

Stranded Pattern A

11
10
9
8
7
6
5
4
3
2
1

Pattern
repeat =
4 stitches

☐ = Beige-Grey Heathered
■ = Pink

Stranded Pattern B

15
14
13
12
11
10
9
8
7
6
5
4
3
2
1

Pattern
repeat =
4 stitches

☐ = Beige-Grey Heathered
■ = Pink

Stranded Pattern C

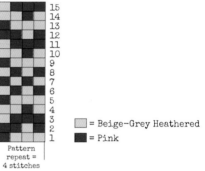

21
20
19
18
17
16
15
14
13
12
11
10
9
8
7
6
5
4
3
2
1

Pattern
repeat =
4 stitches

■ = Pink
☐ = Beige-Grey Heathered

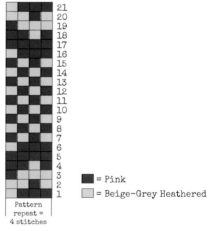

INSTRUCTIONS

CO 64 sts in Beige-Grey Heathered, distribute evenly onto 4 DPNs (16 sts per needle), and join into the round.

For the cuff, work 12 rnds (1 in./2.5 cm) in Cuff Ribbing pattern.

Work the leg in stockinette stitch, beginning with 5 rnds in Beige-Grey Heathered. Now continue in Stranded Pattern A in Beige-Grey Heathered and Pink. Work Rnds 1–11 of the chart once. Then work 4 rnds in Beige-Grey Heathered. Now work Stranded Pattern B in Beige-Grey Heathered and Pink. Work Rnds 1–15 of the chart once. Break the working yarn in Beige-Grey Heathered, and work 10 more rnds in Pink.

Now work a boomerang heel in Pink in stockinette stitch over the 32 sts of Ndls 4 and 1, following instructions on page 179.

Work the foot in stockinette stitch in the round over all sts on all 4 DPNs. Begin with 16 rnds in Pink; then continue in Stranded Pattern C in Pink and Beige-Grey Heathered. Work Rnds 1–21 of the chart once. Break the working yarn in Beige-Grey Heathered. Finish the sock in Pink, beginning toe decreases after 6.9 in./17.5 cm from middle of heel.

Work toe with paired banded decreases according to instructions on page 185. Break the working yarn, and pull the end through to the inside of the sock.

Weave in all ends.

Work the second sock the same way.

WOMEN'S 5½–6
CO 64 sts (16 sts per needle).
Foot: Start with 10 rnds in Pink; then continue as stated in instructions. After 6.3 in./16 cm from middle of heel, begin toe decreases.

WOMEN'S 9–9½, MEN'S 7–7½
CO 68 sts (17 sts per needle).
Foot: Start with 22 rnds in Pink; then continue as stated in instructions. After 7.5 in./19 cm from middle of heel, begin toe decreases.
Note: For Women's 11–12, Men's 8½–9, and larger, 2 skeins of Pink are needed.

WOMEN'S 11–12, MEN'S 8½–9
CO 68 sts (17 sts per needle).
Foot: Start with 28 rnds in Pink; then continue as stated in instructions. After 8.1 in./20.5 cm from middle of heel, begin toe decreases.

MEN'S 10–11
CO 72 sts (18 sts per needle).
Foot: Start with 34 rnds in Pink; then continue as stated in instructions. After 8.7 in./22 cm from middle of heel, begin toe decreases.

From Big

to Small >>>>>>>>>>

SOCKS IN ANY SIZE

This book contains five ready-to-use patterns for children's socks, but you can work many more than that because many of the other patterns from this book can be used for children's socks as well. Smaller colorwork patterns with a pattern repeat of three to six stitches in width are best, since they are small enough for little feet. Larger patterns should be used for socks for longer legs, such as knee-highs. On the following pages, you can find a few ideas on how to combine patterns into new designs. I

will also show you different color combinations that look great not only in tiny sizes but also in larger sizes.

Since especially for the smallest sizes, not a lot of yarn is needed, children's socks are ideal projects for using up remnants. Stitch counts and foot lengths for them can be found in the table on page 170.

For the socks I make, I usually work the leg about the same height as the foot length, which enables me to estimate after how many rounds to start the heel. You can adjust this calculation to your own preferences.

The easiest way to switch out stranded patterns is when the height of the pattern repeat in rows/rounds matches that of one of the ready-to-use instructions. As an example, the pattern repeat for Stranded Pattern C from page 21 (Soxx 3) is six rows/rounds high, the same number of rows as the stranded pattern for Soxx 1. If both gauges match, you have a good indication for how many rounds to work. Socks with this modification are shown on page 156. I have knit them in three instead of four colors, which instantly gives the colorwork pattern a different appearance. If you like it even simpler than that, you can also opt to work these socks in just two colors.

If the desired length has not yet been reached after completion of the colorwork chart, the foot can be made longer by adding a few matching stripes.

Those who like to stay on the safe side can work only the leg in a stranded pattern, and the foot in a solid color or in stripes (see pages 154-55).

I like to combine neutral colors—such as beige, white, off-white, or grey—with brighter ones. Doing so lets the patterns stand out much better. If you are fond of multicolored patterns but don't care for weaving in the ton of ends this process usually entails, you can work the stranded pattern in a long-color-repeat yarn, combined with a contrasting solid color.

SOXX 1

From page 42 in
Child's 11–12.
Knit in Woll Butt Söckli,
super fine (75% wool,
25% nylon; 230 yd./
210 m; 1.75 oz./50 g), in
#24035 White, #41056
Denim Blue, and
#12966 Mustard; with
Stranded Pattern B on
the leg and Stranded
Pattern A on the foot.

SOXX 16 From page 96 in Child's 4–5.
Knit in Woll Butt Söckli, super fine (75% wool, 25% nylon;
230 yd./210 m; 1.75 oz./50 g), in #24035 White and #25349
Tangerine; in Stranded Patterns A and B.

SOXX 15 From page 86 in Child's 4–5.

Knit in Woll Butt Söckli, super fine (75% wool, 25% nylon; 230 yd./210 m; 1.75 oz./50 g), in #41051 Nature, #25350 Apple, and #41056 Denim Blue; with Stranded Pattern C on the leg.

SOXX 25

From page 142 in
Child's 11–12.
Knit in Woll Butt Söckli,
super fine (75% wool,
25% nylon; 230 yd./
210 m; 1.75 oz./50 g), in
#41051 Nature and
#25351 Turquoise; with
Stranded Pattern B on
the leg.

SOXX 3 From page 18 in Child's 4–5.

Knit in Woll Butt Söckli, super fine (75% wool, 25% nylon; 230 yd./210 m; 1.75 oz./50 g), in #24035 White, #25348 Pink, and #41059 Light Grey Heathered; in Stranded Patterns A and C.

SOXX 8 From page 48 in Child's 4–5.

Knit in Woll Butt Söckli, super fine (75% wool, 25% nylon; 230 yd./
210 m; 1.75 oz./50 g), in #41051 Nature, #25348 Pink, and #41056
Denim Blue; in Stranded Pattern A (Rnds 1–4), Stranded Pattern B,
and Stranded Pattern D (Rnds 7–9).

Reinforcement thread

Sock yarn

Sock blocker

Tape measure

Scissors

Cable needle

Yarn guide

Tapestry needle

Row counter

Flexible sock needles

Needle gauge

Stitch markers

DPN sets

Instructions >>>>>

MATERIALS

THE RIGHT YARN

Socks should always be knit from yarns marketed specifically as sock yarns, which are usually a blend of wool combined with about 25–30 percent polyamide (nylon). Fiber content and special treatment make this blend hard-wearing as well as machine washable without felting.

Socks in stranded patterns are best worked from four-ply yarns with a yardage of approximately 230 yd./210 m per 1.75 oz./50 g. In thicker yarns, more elaborate stranded patterns can prove too thick at the instep. Textured patterns from knit and purl stitches, and other single-color patterns or stripes are a good choice for the thicker, six-ply yarn weights. Leftover yarns by different manufacturers may be combined into one project without problems as long as they are of comparable fiber content and yarn weight.

For thinner yarn, heel and toe can be supplemented with same color reinforcement thread, which often comes with it.

Especially pretty and soft are sock yarns in luxurious fiber blends, such as yak, alpaca, or silk; these products create a very unique stitch appearance.

Make sure to choose a high-quality yarn to be able to enjoy your socks for a long time to come.

KNITTING NEEDLES

There are various techniques for knitting socks. Traditionally, DPN sets of five needles are used, which are available in different materials, shapes, and lengths. Deciding whether to use wood, steel, plastic, or bamboo needles depends entirely on personal preference. A large part in the decision process is played by how tightly or loosely one knits.

Bamboo needles are wonderfully lightweight and very yielding while knitting. Their grippy surface makes stitches less likely to slip off but also makes them less suitable for very tight knitters.

Steel needles are somewhat heavier than needles from other materials and have the big advantage of not breaking. However, because of their much slicker surface, they are prone to sliding out of the knitting when working very loosely.

Wooden needles are pleasantly smooth and also lightweight. Sets in smaller sizes often contain a sixth needle, meant as a replacement in case one of the others should break.

Plastic needles are lightweight, too, and flexible. Their tips are more rounded, which makes them less suitable for knitting with multiple colors.

Nowadays, needles are also manufactured in different shapes. Choices include traditional round, triangular, or square-shaped needles.

When it comes to needle length, a wide range is offered. For socks, needles with a length of 6 in./15 cm are best.

As an alternative to DPNs, there are very short circulars, as well as sets of three flexible needles, developed especially for use in sock knitting. These needle types greatly reduce unsightly laddering between needles in the knitted fabric.

NOTIONS

Other tools needed are a tape measure to determine the correct foot length, scissors, and a dull tapestry needle for grafting the toe seam as well as for hiding ends.

For cable patterns, an auxiliary needle or cable needle is also needed. On this needle, stitches to be cabled are held either in front of or behind work.

Stitch markers and row counters make work easier but are not essential. A little homemade loop from a piece of contrasting yarn, a piece of paper, and a pencil will do just as well.

To prevent stitches from sliding off the needles while on the move with your project, specialized stores carry DPN set holders, endcaps, and DPN tubes. Of course, rubber bands may also be used to hold your DPNs together.

When DPN sets of various sizes have accumulated, a needle gauge comes in handy to assemble needles in the required size for a project.

KNITTING BASICS

LONG-TAIL CAST-ON

For socks, I recommend the classic long-tail cast-on, since this cast-on method is elastic but not too loose.

1   For this method, unwind about 24–28 in./61–71 cm of yarn, make a beginning loop or slipknot onto a needle, and tighten it.

2   Lead the yarn tail over your thumb and the working yarn connected to the ball over the outstretched index finger. The needle with the slipknot is between both fingers. Grasp both yarn ends with the free fingers of your left hand to pull them taut.

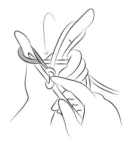

3   Now insert the needle from front to back underneath the strand of yarn in front, and, using the tip of the needle, pull the strand of yarn from the back through. Let the stitch slide off the thumb. Using your thumb, grasp the working yarn again, and pull through to the front. Doing so tightens the stitch, and the yarn goes again over the thumb.

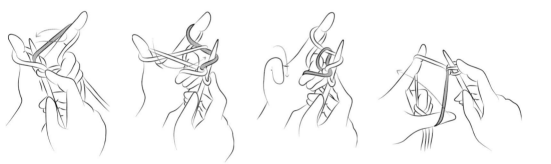

4   Repeat these steps until you've cast on the required stitch count, evenly distributing the total amount of stitches onto four needles. When transitioning to the next needle, keep the yarn taut. Before joining into the round, make sure your cast-on round is not twisted.

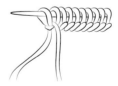

KNIT STITCH

Hold the needle bearing the cast-on stitches in your left hand and the working needle in the right hand with the working yarn behind the needle. Lead the working yarn over the outstretched index finger of the left hand. It can be held taut by winding it several times around the index finger or the pinkie finger.

1 To form a stitch, insert the working needle from front to back into the center of the first stitch, and pull the working yarn through the loop from back to front.

2 Tighten the newly formed stitch on the right needle, and let the stitch of the previous row or round slip from the left needle.

3 Work the following stitches the same way.

Please note: Left-handed knitters hold the needle bearing the cast-on stitches in the right hand and the working needle in their left hand.

PURL STITCH

As with the knit stitch, the needle bearing the cast-on stitches is held in your left hand and the working needle in the right hand. Before working a purl stitch, bring the yarn to the front of the work.

1 With the tip of the right needle in front of the left needle, insert the working needle into the center of the first stitch from right to left, and pull the working yarn through the loop from front to back.

2 Tighten the newly formed stitch on the right needle, and let the stitch of the previous row or round slide from the left needle.

3 Work the following stitches the same way.

Please note: Left-handed knitters hold the needle bearing the cast-on stitches in the right hand and the working needle in their left hand.

Also note: In some Eastern European and Middle Eastern countries, the working yarn is pulled through the stitch in the opposite direction, so knit stitches are mounted on the needle with the other leg in front. This is especially important to consider when working right- or left-leaning decreases. With this way of creating stitches, holes are unavoidable when working a boomerang heel.

STITCHES WORKED THROUGH THE BACK LOOP

KNITTING THROUGH THE BACK LOOP

Insert the needle from right to left into the back leg of the stitch, and knit the stitch, creating a twisted knit stitch.

PURLING THROUGH THE BACK LOOP

Insert the needle from left to right into the back leg of the stitch, and purl the stitch, creating a twisted purl stitch.

GERMAN SHORT ROWS WITH DOUBLE STITCH

After RS rows as well as after WS rows, turn work, and bring the working yarn to the front of the work. Slip the first stitch unworked, simultaneously pulling the working yarn away from you until taut. The stitch is pulled over the needle, with its two legs now sitting on the needle.

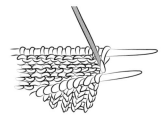  

DECREASES

KNITTING 2 STITCHES TOGETHER (K2TOG)

In the knitted fabric, this decrease leans to the right.

Insert the right needle knitwise into the next two stitches at the same time. Grasp the working yarn, pulling it through both stitches at once.

SLIP-KNIT-PASS (SKP)

In the knitted fabric, this decrease leans to the left.

Insert the right needle knitwise into the following stitch, and slip the stitch onto the right needle. Knit the next stitch, and pass the slipped stitch over the knitted one.

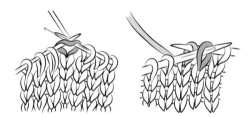

SLIP-SLIP-KNIT (SSK)

Another way of making a left-leaning decrease is to slip-slip-knit. For this, slip 1 stitch knitwise. Now slip the next stitch knitwise too. Insert the left needle from left to right into both slipped stitches at the same time, grasp the working yarn, and pull it through both stitches.

CABLE PATTERNS

In cables, stitches are worked in a switched order. For this approach, hold the required number of stitches on a cable needle either in front of or behind work, depending on whether you want the cable to cross to the left or to the right. Knit the required number of stitches from the main needle; then knit the stitches from the cable needle as instructed.

THE SOCK

FRENCH HEEL WITH PAIRED BANDED TOE DECREASES

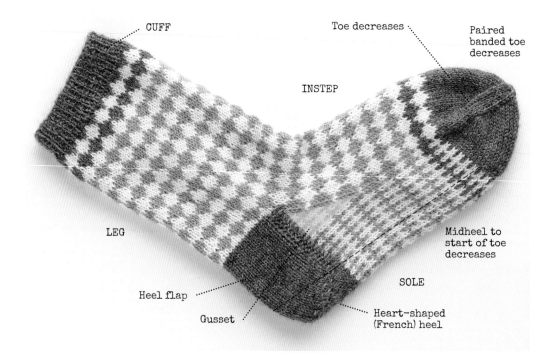

CUFF

Toe decreases

Paired banded toe decreases

INSTEP

LEG

Midheel to start of toe decreases

SOLE

Heel flap

Gusset

Heart-shaped (French) heel

BOOMERANG HEEL WITH ROUNDED TOE

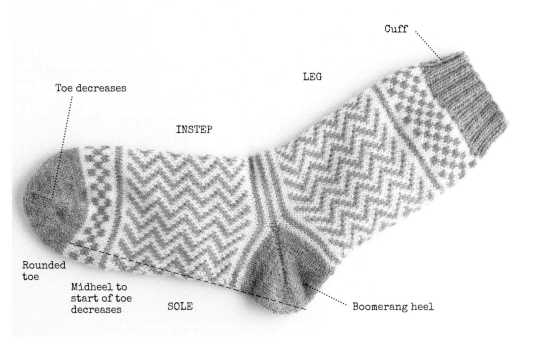

Cuff

LEG

Toe decreases

INSTEP

Rounded toe

Midheel to start of toe decreases

SOLE

Boomerang heel

SIZE CHART

If not otherwise stated, using 4-ply super fine yarn (230 yd./210 m per 1.75 oz./50 g skein)

Size	Child's 1	Child's 2–3	Child's 4–5	Child's 6–7	Child's 8–10	Child's 11–12	Child's 13/ Youth 1	Youth 2–3
CO sts total/per needle for stranded patterns	48/12	48/12	52/13	52/13	56/14	56/14	60/15	60/15
CO sts total/per needle for solid colors and stripes	44/11	44/11	48/12	48/12	52/13	52/13	56/14	56/14
Banded toe foot length from midheel to start of toe decreases	3.75 in./ 9.5 cm	4.3 in./ 11 cm	4.7 in./ 12 cm	5.3 in./ 13.5 cm	5.5 in./ 14 cm	5.9 in./ 15 cm	6.5 in./ 16.5 cm	6.9 in./ 17.5 cm
Round toe foot length from midheel to start of toe decreases	4 in./ 10 cm	4.5 in./ 11.5 cm	5 in./ 12.5 cm	5.5 in./ 14 cm	5.9 in./ 15 cm	6.3 in./ 16 cm	6.9 in./ 17.5 cm	7.3 in./ 18.5 cm
Total foot length	5 in./ 12.5 cm	5.5 in./ 14 cm	5.9 in./ 15 cm	6.5 in./ 16.5 cm	7.1 in./ 18 cm	7.5 in./ 19 cm	8.1 in./ 20.5 cm	8.5 in./ 21.5 cm

Size	Women's 5½–6	Women's 7–8	Women's 9–9½, Men's 7–7½	Women's 11–12, Men's 8½–9	Men's 10–11	Men's 12–13
CO sts total/per needle for stranded patterns	64/16	64/16	68/17	68/17	72/18	76/19
CO sts total/per needle for knit-purl patterns, stripes, etc.	60/15	60/15	64/16	64/16	68/17	72/18
Banded toe foot length from midheel to start of toe decreases	6.3 in./ 16 cm	6.9 in./ 17.5 cm	7.5 in./ 19 cm	8.1 in./ 20.5 cm	8.7 in./ 22 cm	9.3 in./ 23.5 cm
Rounded toe foot length from midheel to start of toe decreases	7.3 in./ 18.5 cm	8 in./ 20 cm	8.5 in./ 21.5 cm	9.1 in./ 23 cm	9.6 in./ 24.5 cm	10.2 in./ 26 cm
Total foot length	8.5 in./ 21.5 cm	9.1 in./ 23 cm	9.6 in./ 24.5 cm	10.2 in./ 26 cm	10.8 in./ 27.5 cm	11.4 in./ 29 cm

THE PERFECT SIZE

How many stitches to cast on to end up with a well-fitting sock depends on various parameters: the yarn weight used, the foot size, the gauge, and the foot circumference.

Every foot is different. For narrow, long feet, fewer stitches may need to be cast on than are listed for the indicated size. Similarly, for short, wide feet, most likely more stitches will need to be cast on than are stated for the actual size. For the patterns in this book, this consideration presents no problem at all, since all pattern repeats are 4 stitches wide, enabling you to switch out stitch counts from smaller or larger sizes.

Stranded patterns can be adapted individually to match the foot length as well—just work fewer or more pattern repeats. If you are not sure, try on your sock-in-progress to check the length from time to time.

With children's socks, it is best to measure the foot. The most reliable method is to have the child stand on a tape measure and measure from the heel to the tip of the longest toe. For the children's socks in this book, foot measurements are listed in addition to shoe sizes.

The leg of the sock can be individually adapted by extending or shortening the color-work pattern.

The patterned socks shown in the photo can be found in Kerstin Balke's first book of socks, *Colorful Knit Soxx,* on pages 82–85.

GAUGE

For a gauge swatch, you may be used to preparing a flat piece about 4.7 x 4.7 in./12 x 12 cm worked in stockinette stitch, which includes purling the wrong side rows for stranded colorwork patterns. This process is rather tedious, and the gauge swatch may not exactly match a piece worked in the round. For this reason, I recommend swatching in the round. With this method, you begin knitting the sock and, instead of counting the rows per 4 in./10 cm, you measure only 2 in./5 cm and then double the row count.

The knitted fabric has to be elastic enough for the finished sock to be pulled on easily.

If your gauge swatch has more stitches than stated in the pattern gauge, you've knitted too tightly and need to switch to a larger needle size. If you have fewer stitches, and your swatch is rather loosely knitted, you need to use a smaller needle size. Specialty stores will carry needle sizes in 0.25 mm increments.

As a rule, the gauge for a stranded pattern will turn out tighter than the gauge for pieces worked in just one color. For patterns containing one section in a stranded pattern and another one in a solid color (such as Soxx 5), different needle sizes can be used to adjust for the discrepancy. The stranded pattern will be worked with a larger needle size than the section in one color will. Stranded patterns are less elastic than solid colors, making it necessary to cast on more stitches overall than for socks worked in one color only.

CUFF AND LEG

CUFF

The cuff's purpose is not only to hold up the sock; it can also be a decorative part.

Ribbed cuffs can be worked in different ways. The two most common ones are "knit 1, purl 1" and "knit 2, purl 2" ribbing. For cuffs in "knit 1, purl 1" ribbing, the stitch count has to be a multiple of 2. After the cast-on, all rounds are worked alternating "k1, p1" until the desired cuff length has been reached.

For a cuff in "knit 2, purl 2" ribbing, the stitch count has to be a multiple of 4. After the cast-on, cuff rounds are worked alternating "k2, p2."

Cabled ribbing produces an especially decorative cuff. For a pattern repeat 4 sts wide, alternate "k3, p1," and cross the cable in every third round. Cables can be crossed either to the left or to the right.

A very pretty and more elastic cuff is created when the knit stitches are worked through the back loop. Since this type of fabric will constrict more, the stitch columns are more pronounced. After the cast-on, all rounds are worked alternating "k1-tbl, p1."

Different cuff ribbings can be chosen according to personal preferences, and the cuff length can be changed as desired as well.

LEG

After the cuff comes the leg, which is worked in stockinette stitch in the round for socks in stranded colorwork patterns, and in the respective charted pattern for socks in knit-purl patterns. It is worked as a straight tube, without increases or decreases. For most socks, the leg length can be varied freely. Socks for the summer are often shorter and look great with sneakers, while traditional winter socks have a longer leg. In the patterns in this book, the leg will often have the same length as the foot. This rule can also be applied when working stranded socks in children's sizes.

STRANDED COLORWORK TECHNIQUE

Knitting stranded colorwork needs a little bit of practice and patience, but it is well worth the effort. With this technique, gorgeous and colorful, customized socks can be knitted.

KNITTING TENSION

Stranded patterns are worked using two or more colors per round, following a colorwork chart. While working in one color, the unused color is carried along in the back of the work. Even tension should be maintained throughout.

If the unused color in the back is pulled too taut, the knitted fabric will constrict. Should this situation happen, it might be necessary to either pull the stitches longer before a color change or switch to a larger needle size. When the float in the unused color is too loose, the knitted fabric will look untidy, and gaps between stitches in different colors may show. In this case, it may help to use a smaller needle size.

To prevent unsightly laddering at the transition, proper tension is especially important in the spots where one needle ends and the next one starts. In these places, pull the working yarn tighter than usual.

For the patterns in this book, the second color is never carried over more than three stitches in the back of the work, which eliminates the need for locking in floats and keeps the fabric more elastic—the more frequently an unused color is woven in, the less elastic the knitted fabric will turn out. If a color stays unused for several rounds, the yarn in this color needs to be crossed with the current color after the third or fourth round of inactivity. Doing so prevents vertical loops on the inside that could get caught when pulling on and taking off the socks. Here, too, make sure to not pull the yarn up too tightly.

A useful tool to help with this is a yarn-stranding guide, the so-called Fair Isle ring. The guide is placed on the index finger, and the different strands of yarn are threaded through the appropriate openings to keep them separated and prevent them from tangling.

HOLDING THE WORKING YARN

There are different ways of holding the yarn. I hold it leading both strands up over the index finger of my left hand. To achieve the correct tension, the front yarn goes down in front of (and the back yarn behind) the middle finger, after which both yarns are held in place with the ring finger and pinkie finger of the same hand. Left-handed knitters need to lead the yarns over their right index finger accordingly.

It is important to always keep the same color in front, since switching between front and back yarn will be noticeable, causing an unruly stitch appearance.

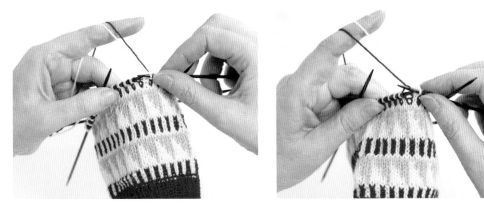

The white strand is in front of the red one.   The red strand is in front of the white one.

The socks shown in these photos can be found in Kerstin Balke's first knit socks book, *Colorful Knit Soxx,* on pages 112–17.

HOW TO READ A COLORWORK OR KNITTING SYMBOL CHART

Colorwork charts and knitting symbol charts are read from bottom to top and from right to left. The pattern repeat is repeated throughout. One box corresponds to one stitch; one chart row equals one round in the knitted piece.

As an example, let's look at the chart for Stranded Pattern B from Soxx 7.

Stranded Pattern B

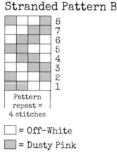

Pattern
repeat =
4 stitches

☐ = Off-White
▨ = Dusty Pink

The pattern starts with two stitches in Off-White, followed by two stitches in Dusty Pink. After the fourth stitch, the pattern repeat starts again, with the first stitch of the repeat. Round 2 starts with one stitch in Dusty Pink, after which two stitches in Off-White are worked. To continue the pattern, "2 stitches in Dusty Pink, 2 stitches in Off-White" are now alternated around, ending the round with "1 stitch in Dusty Pink." For this pattern, the pattern repeat is four stitches wide, requiring an overall stitch count that is a multiple of 4.

When instructions state that the colorwork chart needs to be worked *x* times heightwise, you will start from Round 1 again after completion of Round 8. This process is repeated as often as needed until the pattern has been worked the required number of times.

For socks with textured instead of colorwork patterns, a symbol chart is followed the same way.

A round always begins with the first stitch of the first needle and ends with the last stitch of the fourth needle. In the finished sock, the beginning of the round falls either in the center back of the sock or in the middle of the sole.

HEEL

FRENCH HEEL OR BOOMERANG HEEL?

In many socks, the heel can be switched to a different type, depending on personal preferences. All socks can be worked with a boomerang heel; however, this means that after having worked half of the heel, two rounds will be worked over all stitches, which will disrupt the pattern on the sock. When the foot starts with a stranded colorwork pattern, a French heel can only be added with additional adjustments to the sock. The colorwork patterns in this book do not include incorporated gusset decreases. If needed, the pattern can be adjusted by working the sole in its own pattern, as done with Soxx 8 and 14.

French heels do require more yarn than boomerang heels, which has to be taken into account when substituting heel shapes.

BOOMERANG HEEL

Boomerang heels are worked using the German short rows method with double stitch (see page 166). For the boomerang heel, work over the stitches of the fourth and first needle in stockinette stitch. For this method, combine all stitches onto one needle and divide them into three parts, using stitch markers between sections if needed (see table on page 181).

In the first (upper) part of the heel, you work over the stitches between the two double stitches only, always turning before the double stitch.

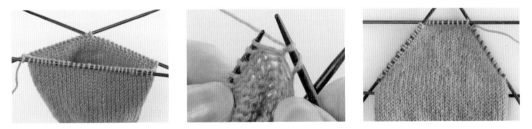

Row 1 (RS): Knit all sts; turn.
Row 2 (WS): Pull out a double st, purl all following sts; turn.
Row 3 (RS): Pull out a double st, knit to double st; turn.
Row 4 (WS): Pull out a double st, purl to double st; turn.

Repeat Rows 3 and 4 until all stitches in the first and last thirds are double stitches; all stitches in the middle third should be single stitches.

Now knit for two rounds over all stitches on all four needles; in the first round, work off both legs of each double stitch as one, when you encounter them.

After this, work the second (bottom) part of the heel over the stitches of the fourth and first needles only.

Row 1 (RS): Knit the sts of the center third and the first st of the left third; turn.
Row 2 (WS): Pull out a double st, purl the sts of the center third and the first st of the right third; turn.
Row 3 (RS): Pull out a double st, knit all sts, including the double st, plus 1 st more; turn.
Row 4 (WS): Pull out a double st, purl all sts, including the double st, plus 1 st more; turn.

Repeat Rows 3 and 4 until both outer sts sit on the needle as double sts.

Evenly distribute the heel sts onto 2 DPNs again, and in the next round, knit both legs of the double sts as one.

Tip: In this heel type, small holes may form between the first and second and the third and fourth needle. This situation happens because the working yarn between the heel stitches and the first or last stitch of the upper foot is not as taut as it should be. Such holes can be avoided with a little trick: After the first part of the heel, when working 2 rounds in stockinette stitch over the sts of all 4 needles, work as follows: After having knit the sts of the first needle, place a stitch marker, and work the first 2 sts of the second needle still using the same needle. Work the sts of the second needle as usual. Now work all but the last 2 sts of the third needle. Slip those 2 sts onto the fourth needle. Work the sts of the fourth needle and place a stitch marker after the 2 additional sts. Work the second half of the heel according to instructions, but work the 2 additional sts before and after the stitch marker and not as double stitch. After having finished the heel section, keep the additional sts for a few more rounds on the first and fourth needles; then move them back to their respective original needles.

STRANDED PATTERNS (4-ply super fine weight; 230 yd./210 m; 1.75 oz./50 g per skein)

Size	Child's 1	Child's 2-3	Child's 4-5	Child's 6-7	Child's 8-10	Child's 11-12	Child's 13-Youth's 1	Youth's 2-3
CO sts total/per needle	48/12	48/12	52/13	52/13	56/14	56/14	60/15	60/15
Heel width, sts Ndl #1 + Ndl #4	24	24	26	26	28	28	30	30
Heel st distribution	8/8/8	8/8/8	8/10/8	8/10/8	9/10/9	9/10/9	10/10/10	10/10/10

Size	Women's 5½-6	Women's 7-8	Women's 9-9½, Men's 7-7½	Women's 11-12, Men's 8½-9	Men's 10-11	Men's 12-13
CO sts total/per needle	64/16	64/16	68/17	68/17	72/18	76/19
Heel width, sts Ndl #1 + Ndl #4	32	32	34	34	36	38
Heel st distribution	10/12/10	10/12/10	11/12/11	11/12/11	12/12/12	12/14/12

KNIT-PURL PATTERNS, STRIPES, ETC. (4-ply super fine weight; 230 yd./210 m; 1.75 oz./50 g per skein)

Size	Child's 1	Child's 2-3	Child's 4-5	Child's 6-7	Child's 8-10	Child's 11-12	Child's 13-Youth's 1	Youth's 2-3
CO sts total/per needle	44/11	44/11	48/12	48/12	52/13	52/13	56/14	56/14
Heel width, sts Ndl #1 + Ndl #4	22	22	24	24	26	26	28	28
Heel st distribution	7/8/7	7/8/7	8/8/8	8/8/8	8/10/8	8/10/8	9/10/9	9/10/9

Size	Women's 5½-6	Women's 7-8	Women's 9-9½, Men's 7-7½	Women's 11-12, Men's 8½-9	Men's 10-11	Men's 12-13
CO sts total/per needle	60/15	60/15	64/16	64/16	68/17	72/18
Heel width, sts Ndl #1 + Ndl #4	30	30	32	32	34	36
Heel st distribution	10/10/10	10/10/10	10/12/10	10/12/10	11/12/11	12/12/12

FRENCH HEEL (HEART-SHAPED HEEL)

For a French heel, work in stockinette stitch over the stitches of the fourth and first needles only. For this method, combine all stitches onto one needle. The first and last 3 stitches are selvedge sts and are always knitted (garter selvedge).

HEEL FLAP

Row 1 (RS): Slip the first st knitwise, knit all sts; turn.

Row 2 (WS): Slip the first st knitwise, knit 2 sts, purl to the last 3 sts, knit 3 sts; turn.

Repeat Rows 1 and 2 until desired height has been reached (see table on page 184); then work the French heel.

HEART SHAPE

The heart shape starts at the middle section of the heel flap sts.

Row 1 (RS): Knit the first half of the heel sts plus the first st of the second half. Work a skp decrease over the following 2 stitches (see page 167), knit 1 st more; turn.

Row 2 (WS): Slip the first st purlwise, purl 3 sts, purl the next 2 stitches together, purl the next st; turn.

Row 3 (RS): Slip the first st knitwise, knit 4 sts, skp the slipped st from the WS row together with the following st, then knit the next stitch; turn.

Row 4 (WS): Slip the first st purlwise, purl 5 sts, purl the slipped st from the WS row together with the following st, then purl the next st; turn.

Continue repeating Rows 3 and 4; always slip the first st of the row and knit or purl the slipped stitch from the previous row together with the following stitch, knit or purl one more stitch, and then turn. With every row worked, one more stitch will be incorporated into the

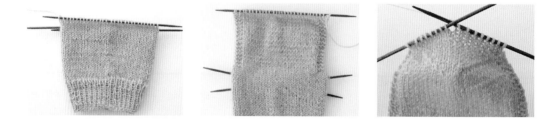

heart-shaped heel. When the selvedge stitches have been reached, the heart-shaped heel has been completed.

PICKING UP STITCHES

After completion of the heart-shaped heel, continue in stockinette stitch in the round. Evenly distribute the heel stitches onto two DPNs. In Round 1, pick up and knit 1 stitch each from every garter stitch selvedge bump of the heel flap.

GUSSET DECREASES

After the heel, you have more stitches on the needles than before; these extra stitches now need to be gradually decreased again. Decreases are worked in every other round on the first and fourth needle. For this method, knit the stitches from the first needle to the last 3 stitches of this needle; then knit together the third- and second-to-last stitch (right-leaning decrease), and knit the last stitch. On the fourth needle, knit the first stitch, and then skp the second and third stitch (left-leaning decrease).

Repeat these decreases until the original stitch count has been reached again.

STRANDED PATTERNS (4-ply super fine weight; 230 yd./210 m; 1.75 oz./50 g per skein)

Size	Child's 1	Child's 2-3	Child's 4-5	Child's 6-7	Child's 8-10	Child's 11-12	Child's 13-Youth's 1	Youth's 2-3
CO sts total/ per needle	48/12	48/12	52/13	52/13	56/14	56/14	60/15	60/15
Heel width, sts Ndl #1 + Ndl #4	24	24	26	26	28	28	30	30
Heel flap, rows	24	24	26	26	28	28	30	30
Sts to pick up on each side	12	12	13	13	14	14	15	15

Size	Women's 5½-6	Women's 7-8	Women's 9-9½, Men's 7-7½	Women's 11-12, Men's 8½-9	Men's 10-11	Men's 12-13
CO sts total/ per needle	64/16	64/16	68/17	68/17	72/18	76/19
Heel width, sts Ndl #1 + Ndl #4	32	32	34	34	36	38
Heel flap, rows	32	32	34	34	36	38
Sts to pick up on each side	16	16	17	17	18	19

SOLID COLORS AND STRIPES (4-ply super fine weight; 230 yd./210 m; 1.75 oz./50 g per skein)

Size	Child's 1	Child's 2-3	Child's 4-5	Child's 6-7	Child's 8-10	Child's 11-12	Child's 13-Youth's 1	Youth's 2-3
CO sts total/ per needle	44/11	44/11	48/12	48/12	52/13	52/13	56/14	56/14
Heel width, sts Ndl #1 + Ndl #4	22	22	24	24	26	26	28	28
Heel flap, rows	22	22	24	24	26	26	28	28
Sts to pick up on each side	11	11	12	12	13	13	14	14

Size	Women's 5½-6	Women's 7-8	Women's 9-9½, Men's 7-7½	Women's 11-12, Men's 8½-9	Men's 10-11	Men's 12-13
CO sts total/ per needle	60/15	60/15	64/16	64/16	68/17	72/18
Heel width, sts Ndl #1 + Ndl #4	30	30	32	32	34	36
Heel flap, rows	30	30	32	32	34	36
Sts to pick up on each side	15	15	16	16	17	18

TOE

TOE WITH PAIRED BANDED DECREASES

In Round 1, on the first and third needle, knit together the third-to-last and second-to-last sts (right-leaning), and on the second and fourth needles, slip the second st, knit the next st, and pass the slipped st over (left-leaning). Work the next 2 rounds even in stockinette stitch without decreases. Repeat the Round 1 decreases in Rounds 4, 6, and 8; then work decreases in every round until only 2 sts remain on each needle (8 sts total). Break the working yarn, thread the end into a tapestry needle and through the 8 sts, and cinch them tightly. Now thread the tail through to the wrong side, and weave it in.

ROUNDED TOE

In Round 1, knit together the third-to-last and second-to-last sts on the first and third needles (right-leaning), and on the second and fourth needles, slip the second st, knit the next st, and pass the slipped st over (left-leaning). Work the next 2 rounds even in stockinette stitch without decreases. Repeat the Round 1 decreases in Rounds 4, 6, and 8; then work decreases in every round until, for shoe sizes Child's 1 to Youth's 3, only 4 sts remain on each needle; for shoe sizes Women's 5½ to Women's 9½ and to Men's 7½, 5 sts; and for shoe sizes Women's 11 and Men's 8½ to Men's 11, 6 sts. Graft the remaining opening in Kitchener stitch (see page 186), and weave in the end.

KITCHENER STITCH

Combine the stitches of the first and fourth needle on one DPN and the stitches of the second and third needle on another. Both needles have to hold the same number of stitches. Place both DPNs on top of each other, break the working yarn (leaving a long tail for grafting), thread it into a dull tapestry needle, and start grafting at the right edge of the piece.

1 Insert the tapestry needle purlwise into the first stitch of the front DPN, and pull the yarn through. Leave the stitch on the DPN.

2 Now lead the tapestry needle through the first stitch of the back DPN knitwise, and pull the yarn through. Leave this stitch on the DPN as well.

3 Now lead the tapestry needle knitwise through the first stitch of the front DPN, and slip the stitch off the DPN. Next, lead the tapestry needle purlwise through the second stitch, pull the yarn through, and leave the stitch on the DPN.

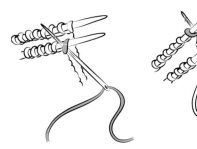  

DPN = double-pointed needle
k = knit
Ndl = needle, DPN
p = purl
rep = repeat
Rnd (s) = Round(s)
RS = right side
skp = slip, knit, purl
st(s) = stitch(es)
WS = wrong side

4   Lead the tapestry needle purlwise through the first stitch of the back DPN, pull the yarn through, and slip the stitch off the DPN. Now lead the tapestry needle through the next stitch of the back DPN knitwise. Pull the yarn through, and leave the stitch on the DPN.

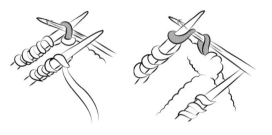

Repeat Steps 3 and 4 until all sts have been grafted. Finish off by threading the tail through to the wrong side and weaving it in.

The Soxx Party

Today is a really gloomy day!
Just plain dull and uninspiring.

Brrr, is it nasty outside! This weather makes you really cranky. Time to cheer up with a pair of cozy socks! With warm feet and a nice cup of tea, everything looks instantly better.

What happened with these? Did the moths have a field day here? Now that's unfortunate! And these colors! They aren't much better than the disgusting muck outside!

That won't do! No way these drab grays can stay in the house, let alone on my feet! Where would we end up with that?

Hmmm! But now what? My feet are still freezing.

Hey, what's that? My trusty old wool basket! Let's see what we can find here.

Oh, how wonderful! This fantastic red, that delicate green, the heavenly pastel blue, and that sunny yellow! I didn't know I had all these great colors in my basket. That's like a whole rainbow!

About the Author

Kerstin Balke, aka Stine & Stitch, learned to knit at age six from her grandmother. Since then, her output has included sweaters, cardigans, scarves, hats, and even delicate tablecloths, but her true passion is sock knitting.

For several years now, Kerstin has been designing her own patterns—most often colorful, sometimes also perfectly subtle, but always using multiple colors.

On her blog (www.stineundstitch.blogspot.de) and on Instagram as @stine_und_stitch, she showcases her newest creations and shares sock knitting tips and tricks.

With her husband and their two daughters, Kerstin lives in Germany, between Hamburg and Lübeck.

ACKNOWLEDGMENTS

Thank you to my family for enduring my never-ending chatter about socks, colors, and patterns, and for putting up with WIP (work-in-progress) clutter all over the place, with virtually no complaints.

To my test knitters, whose works can be admired on Instagram, for their speedy execution of my instructions and wonderful feedback. Without your diligence, numerous mistakes would have been able to sneak in! Thanks, Barbara (@thoni_knits), Claudia (@reetseelig), Etha, Isa (@luisa_wolkenschein), Kirsten (@knightlyart), Konstanze (@lilliliebtlollis), Lydia (@lydiafisch), Sabine (@hexbexhamburg), Steffi (@lille_boat), and Svenja (@foerdefaden).

For yarn support, I would like to thank Lang Yarns (www.langyarns.com), MEZ Crafts (www.schachenmayr.com), Lana Grossa (www.lana-grossa.de/en/), Gustav Selter & Co. KG, (www.addi.de/en/), Buttinette (www.buttinette.com), and ducathi (www.ducathi.de).